Harold Sharp

THE BEST IN FAMILY READING
Choice Books
Dept. I, P. O. Box 472
Harrisonburg, VA 22801
We Welcome Your Response

GOD HEALED THEM...

— "Perhaps a year — not more," the doctor told him. But twenty years later, he is enjoying a vigorous retirement.

— She was confined to a wheelchair, growing "stiff as a board" from progressive, incurable arthritis . . . yet rose and walked within minutes of being anointed and prayed for.

— The young man hours away from death from encephalitis . . . the boy doomed to an invalid's life by rheumatic fever . . . the girl with one leg shorter than the other . . . the partially blind young wife —

These are only a few of the people who tell their own stories of suffering, of the powerlessness of medical methods to help, of the power of prayer and healing. Too often derided by skeptics, divine healing is shown to be indisput-
able fact by th__ __ty-four first-
__ __s . . . firm
__d.

GOD HEALED ME

ROBERT J. BAKER

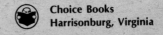

Choice Books
Harrisonburg, Virginia

GOD HEALED ME

A Choice Book published by Herald Press for Mennonite Broadcasts, Inc. Manufactured by Keats Publishing, Inc.

Copyright © 1974 by Herald Press, Scottdale, Pa. 15683

All rights reserved

Library of Congress Catalog Card Number: 74-17801

International Standard Book Number: 0-8361-1755-7

Choice Books edition, 1974

CHOICE BOOKS are distributed exclusively by Mennonite Broadcasts, Inc., Harrisonburg, Va. 22801. The word "Choice" and the corresponding symbol are registered in the United States Patent Office.

Printed in the United States of America

ACKNOWLEDGMENTS

My grateful thanks,
to Marge McGinnis, who typed the manuscript,
to Paul M. Miller, who provided a bibliography,
to each and every person who supplied material,
words of encouragement,
words of warning, and
to my family. To write is a lonely task. I thank
my family, and especially my good wife, Anna Mae,
who permitted me those long hours of solitude
that I demanded.
To God be the final thanks, to God be the glory!

CONTENTS

SECTION THREE: THE EPILOGUE

SECTION ONE

THE EXPLANATION

WHAT I HAVE TRIED TO DO

In this book I am presenting for God's honor and glory a collection of incidents which I feel speak to the subject of divine healing.

I know many physicians, surgeons, nurses, dentists, laboratory technicians, and a variety of therapists in both the physical and mental areas of health science. I value and respect their education, research, and experience. I accept the skill of such men and women who have dedicated their lives to both easing and eliminating the sicknesses which beset mankind.

And yet I firmly believe that all healing is of God. The physician may set the stage for such healing, yet he cannot command the bruised flesh, the torn tissue, the shattered bone to restore itself to perfection. There are times when the medical specialist must confess that he has reached his limitations. But God is not bound by such limitations. Sometimes God applies the balm of Gilead when man despairs of cure.

Who I Am

I have taught science for more than twenty-five years in the public schools of Indiana. I received my higher education in five reputable universities and colleges. I present this book with the full knowledge that divine healing often seems to violate logical, sequential thinking based on the natural laws of cause and effect.

What This Book Is Not

The divine healing reported in this book is noncommercial in nature. It is not due to prayer cloths, water from the Jordan River, or financial bargains made with God. The cures, the deliverances, have come because of man's simple faith, the anointing with oil, the laying on of hands, the healing ministry of the Holy Spirit, God demonstrating His power over Satan.

This book is not a call for the reader to discard his medicine, to cancel his doctor's appointment, to request discharge from the hospital. If I pray for safety as I travel, God does not in turn ask me to cut the brake cables on my car to prove that I have a valid faith in Him.

A Simple Statement of Faith

This book is a simple call for a simple faith in a God who cares for every little sparrow that falls, a God who cares for me. It is a call to couple God's healing ministry at the hands of man with His healing ministry at the hands of His Holy Spirit. It is not a call for the one to refute the other.

The common saying, "Man's extremities are God's possibilities," applies to the experiences related in this book. In many of the cases, there is no apparent scientific reason why the person was healed. In some situations, the case was "hopeless," non-treatable in the sight of man. Fortunately, "hopeless" is not found in God's dictionary.

Some Limitations, Some Acknowledgments

I am quite conscious that many illnesses are psychosomatic in nature, that the will to live, faith in the creative work of the healer, temporary remissions of certain afflictions, a faulty preliminary diagnosis, all present significant factors that need to be considered where divine healing is claimed.

If we are not careful, however, in the process of explaining away divine healing, we may explain away God.

I am convinced that at times God allows us to go beyond our faith in physician and penicillin. His infinite wisdom bridges the gap, the healing streams flow down, and the Great Physician performs a work of physical grace in the life of one of His children. This miracle of physical healing is no greater than the miracle of spiritual healing which every Christian must acknowledge as truth and reality for his own life.

No Magic Formula

I have included in this book cases where God has not healed, at least physically. It seemed right to do so. I doubt if Jesus healed everyone He met while upon this earth.

Why does God not heal in such cases? I do not know. Perhaps it is because He is a God who sees the total pattern that is being woven in all of life, while I only see what seems to be the misplaced thread.

No magic formula emerges to assure divine healing. I did not find that God healed only after so many hours of prayer or so many days of fasting. God does not seem to demand an anointing with oil ceremony or the laying on of hands by Spirit-filled men, although often the two practices were involved in the healings. God seemed to tailor His preconditions to the case at hand.

Or Think of It Like This

Even in the cases where the sick remained sick, where the dying died, I found healing.

When pain-racked physical bodies succumbed to the ravages of disease to which God did not choose to respond with healing, paradoxical as it sounds, there was complete and glorious victory over the affliction. It was a type of healing to which every Christian can testify. For we know that when this corruptible body of ours puts on incorruption, when this mortal puts on immortality, we will experience healing in the most permanent, eternal sense of the word.

Undoubtedly there are people who, upon the death of a loved one, curse God and are themselves ready to die. But among Christians I interviewed who had lost a loved one there was a fragrance of heavenly perfume that far exceeded the scent of earthly burial spices.

It's a Personal Matter

One's belief or disbelief in divine healing pivots around one's answer to several questions. Is the Bible true? Was Jesus actually a miracle worker, the Son of God? Was Jesus' promise in John 14:12 which testifies that His followers shall perform even greater works than those which He did still germane for us of today?

Each person must answer those questions personally, thus determining what size his God shall be. For me, personally, the questions are all answered by a clear cut "Yes." I believe that God answers prayer. I believe that God heals. A writer on such a subject must have an opinion. And no reader can truthfully remain neutral. You either believe or you do not believe.

Words to the Skeptics

A few words to the skeptics of divine healing, especially those richly steeped in science. I also am science saturated. In spite of our need to be open-minded, our studies in the laws that govern matter and its interaction with other matter limits that very openness we would profess to hold. It is a hurdle that often we cannot leap, a mental block that short circuits our thinking, the concrete that locks our minds into a bigoted rigidity.

We in science remain leery, running scared of any thought lying outside the sacred realism of Newton, Copernicus, and Einstein, Inc. For such skepticism we must pay. I would remind all doubting Thomases, however, of the reputable studies and research that progresses at present in such fields as acupuncture, parapsychology, and psychokinesis. The ridiculous of yesterday is being looked at afresh today because of the effect it may have upon tomorrow.

Cannot we have our cake and eat it too? Those who insisted that light had to travel in only one of two ways, either waves or particles, found out that their separate dogmas only isolated them from the truth. The dogmatic scientist of today who scorns and scoffs at the idea that there is a God who heals, may find himself the Ptolemy of tomorrow. I believe in medicine. I believe in God. I believe the two are compatible.

To God Be the Glory

As one would expect, not everyone has encouraged me to write this book. A few have suggested that it not be written. The question of my credibility for the future is raised.

I am somewhat amused at the latter. Frankly, I would like to think that I no longer need the placebo of status, the tranquilizer of man's approval, the stimulant of acclaim. As I grow older, I am becoming a good deal more interested in what God thinks of me than what people think of me.

I recognize that before this book is in print, some of the cases involved may have already left this earth to be with God. And on their death certificates may appear the very ailment from which they testify in this book that they have been delivered.

God does not promise us eternal life upon this earth. His time is not our time. He delivered David from the hand of Saul, from the claw of the bear and the lion, but eventually he called David to be with Him. For fifteen years God extended the life of Hezekiah, but not forever. Lazarus lives in heaven, not Bethany. The healed demoniac no longer testifies on the shores of the Sea of Galilee concerning the healing touch of Jesus.

I personally do not scorn God's healing for the moment on this earth, and how I praise Him for the healing that shall last forever and forever throughout eternity.

To God be the glory!

MY MODE OF OPERATION

Leads concerning cases of divine healing to be considered came through notices in church papers, announcements at workshops and conferences, suggestions supplied by concerned peoples, and personal contacts by the author. Undoubtedly I failed to hear of genuine cases that should have been included, and possibly I have included some cases that others may question. The faith and confidence of each person whose story is told in this book is sincere.

Each case considered was supplied with a preliminary survey form for the gathering of initial information.

Telephone contacts often followed and where possible personal interviews were conducted.

A form was sent to physicians who may have been involved in the care of the person testifying of divine healing.

Not all physicians returned the form, and in some cases the physician was deceased. A physician's name listed as a witness following any account indicates his agreement that it is a case of divine healing by his evaluation and the criteria we set up. A number of physicians marked their survey form "questionable" in regard to whether the case under review should be considered as divine healing. Their names, of course, could not be included as witnesses. Some cases are included where consulting physicians thought the healing could not be classified by our definition as one of "divine healing."

Some physicians admitted freely their belief in divine healing; some commented that all healing is divine; several suggested that the book not be written.

I did not feel that the failure to receive medical documentation necessarily meant that the case should no longer be considered. In fact, in some cases it was impossible to make contact with medical personnel involved.

A copy of each case as written up was sent to the person involved for corrections. A release form was signed by the person healed and returned to me.

Each person who testified to divine healing was asked to supply the names and addresses of two witnesses who knew the person's ailment and also was in agreement with the facts of the case. Readers desiring additional information may write to such witnesses.

Cases included in this book where persons have not been restored to health, of course, contain no witnesses. Many witnesses are available, however, to testify that these persons have found peace with God as they submitted to His will in their life.

The addresses of those whose experiences are included in the chapters which follow are given at the back of the book.

A selected bibliography of references on the subject of divine healing has been generously provided by Professor Paul M. Miller of the Mennonite Biblical Seminary.

Our sincere thanks to all who responded to our call to provide material for this book.

SECTION TWO

THE EVIDENCE

1 THE DIAGNOSIS WAS LEUKEMIA

MY HUSBAND was the one appointed to break the news to me. It was surprising news, shocking and frightening news.

On June 27, 1968, we had our third child, our first daughter. At that time we thought all was well, but when I took the baby back to the doctor, he said my blood test, which had been done in the hospital, was "low" and that I should go back for retesting.

I thought little of it, but at the hospital I found more tests were involved than before. It seemed strange, but I was not worried. I did seek additional information from my doctor, but he told me that Elvin, my husband, had an appointment with him in the next day or so and perhaps it could be discussed further with him at that time.

So Elvin broke the news to me at the hospital. Then

Mrs. Elvin Martin, mother of four, lives near Kinzers, Pennsylvania, a small village in Lancaster County. For hobbies she enjoys sewing and reading. Her husband operates a dairy farm.

I understood about the retesting, about the extra tests.
Elvin said, "Lois, the tests show you have leukemia."

I thought, "Oh, no! This can't be happening to me."
But it was.

My immediate reaction was despondency. I did not
fear death, but like any mother, I thought of the three
children who needed me.

My doctor was honest. I wanted it that way. Although
I was on medication, he made no promises. I understood
I had acute stem cell leukemia, diagnosed by a bone
marrow examination. It was a very malignant form of
leukemia of a type that progresses rapidly and normally
leads to an early death. It was difficult to be optimistic.

For me, as for many, the medical doctor was the
ultimate help and relief for man's illnesses. I have had
only respect and admiration for the skills practiced by
medical personnel. So you can imagine how I felt when
they admitted the difficulty of my case. The people who
had the best chance to save me were raising some serious
questions about their ability to bring me through. It
was like having two strikes on you and a fast ball coming
up.

I grasped at straws. Some people said vitamins and
health foods help counteract leukemia. So I tried them.
But inside I longed for greater, more substantial help.
I wanted something I could believe in, not something
someone else said was good.

It was a time of wavering, of questioning, of doubting,
of discouragement. There was no promise in medication,
in vitamins, in stone ground flour, in alfalfa sprouts.
I wanted something to set my sights on, to aim at, a
target that could be counted on to stand still. My world
was shifting about me. I needed something to cling to,
something that was higher than I.

And then I found it. The idea of an anointing service
for my healing surfaced in my mind. My husband and

I were Christians. We were members of a denomination
that professed to believe in divine healing. Could God
do what the doctors could not do, provide the anchor
I needed? Could He heal me?

I have always believed in divine healing, but I always
believed in it for other people. Did I believe in it for
myself? I did. I asked that I be anointed for my healing.

The service was conducted in my home. My bishop,
Clair Eby, along with deacon Willis Hershey were in
charge. It was a simple affair. Only my parents and
Elvin's parents were there. It was a period of sharing,
of praying, of seeking God's will. And then the oil was
gently poured upon my head, a symbolic action of our
confidence in God, symbolizing also how we felt His
love was poured out upon us.

What happened? I had the inner confidence that this
was the thing to do. I knew from that moment I would
be healed. The assurance that I sought came with gen-
tleness, yet firmness.

Several weeks passed. There was further testing, this
time by God instead of the doctors. I came down with
pneumonia.

I was very ill. For nearly two weeks I ran a fever
of 104 to 105. The doctor came to our home on Tuesday
and Wednesday of that first week. And when he left,
he said, "If you need me, call me."

I lay there, a bit lightheaded, and I thought I heard
him saying by that offer, "I'll come, but a doctor can
only do so much."

The leukemia had been more than enough, but now
came the pneumonia. People who knew me were concerned. They worried about me, about what would
happen if I died, how Elvin would get along with the
three children. They said as much, and what was not
said, I sensed.

The decision was made to take me to the hospital

again. There I was given several pints of blood and medication. The fever subsided.

One day a specialist came into the room to speak to me. He told me that the leukemia was no worse, if anything a little better. It was the first of the good news, the beginning proof of my healing for which I had trusted God.

His news was actually no surprise to me. Since my anointing I felt different, buoyant. In my pneumonia experience, I still clung to that act of faith on my part, my calling for the prayers of the elders of the church, my request that the biblical injunction of James be carried out in my life.

It must have been the Lord continually reassuring me. I knew enough about this type of leukemia that my chances for living were slim. The doctors had never given me any encouragement. The prognosis was always dark. With life there was hope, but with leukemia, not much.

I was in the hospital a week, then discharged. I do not remember much about that week and the one that went before, except that which I have related. I did have some visitors, limited in number, but I remember little of what was said. I was so weak that those two weeks were almost like a dream. I just faintly remember who was in to see me, and hardly anything of their conversation. I suppose that some of them thought they were paying their last respects to me while I was alive. But I knew better.

From that time on I gradually regained my strength. I know that my home congregation, the Hershey Mennonite Church, was much in prayer for my recovery. And many others also were interceding for me at God's throne.

One thing I did remember about those days of recovery. A visitor said to me, "When you get company, don't wait for them to cheer you up; you cheer them up."

And since I had God's assurance of my recovery, I could do that. Paul said he could do all things through Christ who strengthened him. I felt the same way. I have tried to remain optimistic all my life.

I feel that last statement is extremely important for the Christian. In the midst of suffering, of trouble, we must look up. We must trust God. We must be eternally hopeful. I have had no more burdens than what God thought I was able to bear. He knows the weight of the load we carry. And He cares. He does not build a hedge around us to protect us, but He does surround us with His blanket of love. And in our coldest moment, that love warms us.

Even when my eyesight failed shortly after my siege with pneumonia, when I could not see to read, when people became a blur just a short distance away, I clung to God.

And He has honored that faith. Doctors said my eyes were damaged by the severity of the illness. But today I can see as well as ever. If my eyesight was damaged, God healed it.

It has now been five and a half years since I was diagnosed as having leukemia, five years since I was so seriously ill in the hospital. People are still coming to me and asking how I am, especially since having another baby. It just seems like they can hardly believe I am well.

After telling them I am feeling fine, and the blood tests show everything to be okay, they often say, "Well, I was praying for you." I think it really makes them feel as though they had a part in my healing. And I believe they did, because if it weren't for the many prayers that went up on my behalf, I don't know if I would be here. I know it strengthened my faith and the faith of all those who were praying to know God still answers prayer. My healing is proof of that.

We did not have insurance at that time to cover our

huge medical bills. All the Sunday school classes in
our church, from the youth class on up, gave us a love
gift. It meant so much to us, not just that our obligations
were paid, but that they had that much love for us.
I know that the Lord will bless them for it.

My prayer is that my experience will bring honor
and glory to the Lord and not to me or anyone else.

Praise God!

Witnesses:

Mr. and Mrs. Paul H. Weaver
13 N. Conestoga View Drive
Akron, Pennsylvania 17501

Mrs. Ray Beyer
Route 4
Lititz, Pennsylvania 17543

Dr. John Rutt, M.D.
Intercourse, Pennsylvania 17534

2 RISE UP AND WALK

• Kate M. Miller

IT HAS BEEN SUGGESTED by some church authorities that a case of divine healing should be considered authentic only after a period of five years has elapsed from the time of healing. I suppose this is to eliminate some of the psychological "healings" where a person is emotionally keyed up and "feels he is healed." In a few days that emotional high wears off and the person is back where he was before.

My healing took place on February 11, 1940. I have claimed God's healing for a period of thirty-four years. So, I seem to have satisfied the time requirement laid down by such people.

I had been in failing health for some time, and by January, 1939, I was no longer able to do my housework.

Kate Miller, the wife of Paul R. Miller, who served as a Mennonite pastor until his recent retirement, lives in Sarasota, Florida. She has often shared her testimony of God's healing and is happy to do so again.

Although accompanied by heart trouble, the ailment that incapacitated me was spinal arthritis. And by March of 1939 I was in bed and could not so much as move my toes.

The doctor gave his honest prognosis, suggesting that the disease was progressive, that it would continue to worsen, that eventually I would become as "stiff as a board." I was given medication to relieve the pain, and this along with daily treatments under an ultraviolet lamp was all he could offer.

Most of us fail to appreciate the simple functioning of a joint in our body, the ability to flex a muscle and move an arm or leg. How I wished for that ability in the spring of 1939.

After several months of nearly total bed confinement, I begged my husband and the hired girl to get me out of bed and help me walk again. Against his better judgment he did and, after nearly six weeks of painful struggling, I was able to walk along the walls. By clinging to chairs I could fight my way about. But I certainly was not healed.

The spinal arthritis continued to twist my spine. Eventually I could not bow my head nor raise my hands. I lost even the ability to struggle around the house. I could not sit on a chair, but had to lie in bed or be placed on a lawn chair. I stood up to eat my meals. I was becoming like a wooden soldier. It was often impossible to sleep at night without sedatives.

And my heart condition worsened. The attacks continued, increasing in severity. One night I had such a hard attack that I knew I could not last much longer. I asked my husband if he would request our bishop, O. N. Johns, to come and anoint me in accordance with James 5.

My husband had thought for some time that this should be done, but wanted the request to come from me. He rejoiced at my wish, that I had fulfilled the biblical injunction where it says in James 5:14, "Is any sick among you? Let *him* call for the elders of the church; and let them pray over him, anointing him with oil in the name of the Lord." The "him" refers to the person who is sick. We didn't know anything about women's liberation in those days, and the "him" didn't bother me at all. I just knew I wanted to ask the Lord for healing.

We arranged to have the anointing service on a Sunday afternoon, February 11, 1940. We invited our local ministers and their wives, my sister and family. Of course, our bishop, O. N. Johns, and his wife were also there. The service was set for 2:30 and we had asked the church to be in prayer at that same time.

We spent some time in scripture reading, prayer, and singing. We confessed our faults one to another as the James scripture suggests. It was a time of honest sharing. I was lying on the davenport, my husband, Paul, sitting at the end of it. Everyone around the circle offered a prayer. My prayer was for healing, but I prayed also, "Not my will, but Thine be done."

The bishop asked me several questions concerning my belief in the James passage, questions that drew from me the measure of my faith in God's ability to heal.

Then the group gathered around me for the laying on of hands and Brother O. N. Johns anointed me with oil in the name of Jesus Christ. There was prayer again. I felt I was healed immediately.

I debated, however, whether I should get up while my company was still present, or wait until they went home.

There was more singing. I asked them to sing the doxology as my praise song. While they were still singing, I asked for my shoes. I sat up and put them on.

Paul took my hand and I walked over and sat down on a dining room chair—something I had been unable to do for nine months. I was completely healed. It was instantaneous.

No words could express my joy. I had been a shut in for thirteen and one-half months. Doctors had offered no hope for my recovery. To know that I was suddenly healed almost overcame me. I laughed, cried, and talked. I was so happy, I could hardly contain myself.

All of us in that room experienced the power of God. Bishop O. N. Johns later testified, "Immediately after having anointed this sister in Christ, I had full assurance she was healed. If it had not been for Mennonite modesty, I would have taken her by the hand and said, 'Sister, rise up and walk. Thy faith hath made thee whole.'"

I walked to the porch to bid our guests good-bye. The next morning I did our family washing. I never had a pain.

When I went to church the next Sunday, some people were shocked to see me. Friends came to see what a wonderful thing God had done. From people I never knew, I received letters marveling at God's healing power.

My doctor, now deceased, waited a week, then came and picked up the ultraviolet lamp he had arranged for me to use. I met him a year later at a wedding and he remarked that I looked healthier than he did. I could only praise God.

The community was electrified. Unsaved people came to me asking if our bishop could not anoint them. They thought it was the man. It wasn't a man; it was God. I always carefully explained to them the conditions God laid down, the need of a complete surrender on their part. No one should ask to be anointed unless he is completely yielded to Christ and fully submissive to

God's will. Only then can there be sufficient faith for his healing.

As I look back these many years, I recall how often my husband, Paul, read out of the book of Job during that trying period. Job suffered, but testified after his healing in Job 42:2, "I know Thou canst do everything."

I believe that. God did everything for me.

Thank You, Lord.

Witnesses:

O. N. Johns
Louisville, Ohio 44641

Venus Hershberger
Route 2
Sugarcreek, Ohio 44681

3 WE CALL IT A MIRACLE

● Glen Dale Miller

I WAS NOT COMPLETELY MYSELF that day in the hospital when I came back from x-ray. But I was conscious enough to know that I was very, very sick. It was only my first day in the hospital, and in my mind I wondered if I would leave it alive.

My wife was waiting in my hospital room and we had a few bittersweet moments together. I remember telling her how I was sorry to leave her alone—a young wife to care for our son, but to me it seemed that God was calling me home. And at age 23, I wasn't anxious to go. Half of our Voluntary Service term in Corpus Christi, Texas, had now been completed, but it looked as if the other half would never be finished.

The trouble began on December 19, 1972, just six

The First Mennonite Church of Middlebury, Indiana, is the home congregation of Dale and June Miller. At the time of this writing he is serving in the public schools of Corpus Christi, Texas.

days before Christmas. I had not been feeling well for several weeks, due mainly to an upper respiratory infection, but that morning new problems appeared. I experienced numbness in my legs, a headache, backache, and dizziness. These symptoms bothered my wife, June, and myself.

We decided to consult our doctor for medication. After examining me, the doctor gravely turned to me and said, "I believe you have encephalitis."

I still didn't understand the seriousness of it, in spite of his grave manner. So he explained further. He looked directly into my eyes, and answered my questions like this: "You may get better. You may get worse. You may die."

From the doctor's office I went to the hospital carrying a temporary diagnosis of encephalitis. This is simply a fancy word for inflammation of the brain tissues. As an assistant principal in the Lamar Elementary School of Corpus Christi, I felt disturbed that my "thinking system" was involved. I knew now that my problem was serious. But it was steadily to grow even worse.

By evening of that first day in the hospital I was weaker and knew it. At first I was not required to be in bed all the time, but by the second day new orders confining me to bed came from the doctor. I had broken several glasses simply because I did not have the strength to move the glass of water from my bed stand to my mouth.

Although I talked to June during the next two days, Tuesday and Wednesday, I have little recollection of it. Reality was a come and go affair, mostly go. I knew little of the spinal taps that were being taken.

On Wednesday when June came to see me, I was still weaker. The nurses were feeding me. I was only partly coherent. I know June was alarmed, although she tried not to show it. We had some moments alone in the room. We talked, prayed, and cried together. And we were afraid.

On Thursday morning I was taken to intensive care and June was called to the hospital, fearing that I had died or was dying. An emergency tracheotomy was performed, so I could breathe through a tube in my throat. My breathing which had been labored, now was easier.

When June asked the doctors (at this point I had five, including a neurologist) if the tracheotomy would be permanent, they replied, "Not if he lives."

Then the diagnosis was changed to meningoencephalomyelitis. This is a disease that affects the central nervous system, involving the spinal cord and brain. My body was completely paralyzed except for thinking and breathing, the latter now relieved by the tracheotomy. I was being given oxygen at intervals. The doctors advised June to contact my parents at Middlebury, Indiana. June was being forewarned, prepared.

My wife went home that Thursday night deeply depressed. She called a friend, Grace Miller, a former Voluntary Service worker in Premont, Texas. Grace seemed unable to console June. Later that evening Grace found James 5:14-15 in her Bible and knew that was the answer, but decided it was too late to call. She prayed that June would find that scripture.

At home June searched her Bible for comfort, for direction. And the next morning she was led to that passage of scripture that suggests calling for the elders of the church and anointing with oil.

She immediately called Paul Conrad, pastor of the Prince of Peace Mennonite Church in Corpus Christi. That Friday morning twelve of my Christian friends came to the hospital. Only Pastor Conrad and June were allowed in the isolation room. The rest prayed outside in the hall.

Paul anointed me with oil. June and I never leaned on God or other people as much as we did that day.

I vaguely remember the anointing, but when they left the room I sensed more peace and quietness than I ever had before. I closed my eyes then, barely realizing what had taken place, expecting to die. I had told June earlier my only regrets were that I had to leave her and Jeremy (age 1) by themselves, but that I was ready to go.

But June refused to believe that I was going to die and said that God had revealed to her that I would be completely healed and we had to have faith. Her whole outlook had changed.

The next morning I opened my eyes, expecting to be in heaven. In the seconds that followed, I realized the crisis was over, that God had reversed the events of the last few days, and that I was going to recover.

That same day movement returned to my toes, and in the following days other parts of my body "came back to life." I was experiencing a miracle. On Sunday the tube in my trachea was removed and the incision began to heal.

My bladder was still not functioning a week later though the doctor had removed my catheter twice before without success. My eyes were still blurry and I had double vision at times. I had very little coordination and fell to the floor on one occasion. I began to think perhaps this was to be the extent of my recovery, but my wife kept telling me we must not lose faith.

That night I prayed that God would give me some small sign to reassure me that I would be healed completely. The following morning the doctor said we would try to get my bladder functioning again. There was success. God proved His faithfulness!

After one month in the hospital, I returned home. I rested for three more weeks, then I returned to my job as fifth grade teacher in the classroom. I was still weak, but my strength came back in the next several weeks.

After I was out of the hospital I heard about many prayer groups that had interceded for me. Our home congregation formed a prayer chain. Our congregation in Corpus Christi had many special prayer sessions. Friends of ours attending other churches came to God requesting my healing. Sunday school classes in Indiana and Ohio lifted special offerings. More than a hundred individuals sent cards, letters, and called long distance. These gestures of concern I now appreciate more than I can express.

At one point during my recovery, while still in the hospital, I said to my doctor, "I feel that we had God on our side."

"I know you have," he admitted.

Then he added, "You should thank the good Lord for what you have."

Oh, we do, we do! Thank You again, Lord. Thank You for Your healing hand!

Witnesses:
    Paul Conrad
    2009 Harvard
    Corpus Christi, Texas 78416

    June Miller
    1821 Horne Road
    Corpus Christi, Texas 78416

4 ENABLING GRACE

● Helen Good Brenneman

I HAVE LIVED with multiple sclerosis for over ten years. I have been anointed with oil. I have been prayed for by countless people. A faith healer came to our home, laid his hands upon me, and prayed for my recovery. I have not been healed. A flicker of hope wavers within me, a hope that I will improve, even that complete healing will come. Yet, in general, I know that it is not the nature of the disease. I live by God's enabling grace. Each day He measures out to me the grace I need for the day. It is always enough.

Multiple sclerosis placed me in a wheelchair, at first infrequently, now most of the time. In 1972, I found it necessary to use the wheelchair in the house. Pre-

Helen Good Brenneman of Goshen, Indiana, is a prominent and prolific Mennonite writer, the author of *Meditations for the New Mother, Meditations for the Expectant Mother, My Comforters, The House by the Side of the Road,* and *Ring a Dozen Doorbells.* She is a frequently sought speaker for women's groups.

viously I had been able to move throughout the home by clinging to furniture and using crutches. Now, I use a wheelchair. My ailment has also seriously affected my vision, making reading almost impossible. But I refuse to blame God. I refuse to believe that God does not heal. What He has done for me in my illness, for my family, the grace He has given, far exceeds the wonder of healing. Frankly, I feel that it takes more faith to accept my illness with its physical limitation than it would to be healed. I praise God for the faith that He has given me, a faith that is guaranteed for life. It is my medicine.

I am a housewife, the mother of four, a writer. I do freelance writing, I write on assignment. When I was only twelve years old I was a columnist for the *Washington Star,* a daily paper of Washington, D.C. It was true that it was only the junior page, a section devoted to young people, but I wrote. Writing is a part of my ministry, a ministry in which I am more involved at present than I ever was. And without this illness, I am not certain if I would have had time for the writing that I love to do. I know that my writing has been both directed and used of God.

Perhaps my physical problems and limitations have enabled me to write with insights denied to others. A number of the books and articles that I have authored were possible only because of what I have experienced, areas in which I have suffered and been blessed. I believe a writer must write of that which he knows best. I know of handicaps. I know the joy of the Lord. And so I write of that which has touched me, which has blessed me.

Please do not think of me as a saint. I am not. Multiple sclerosis is a disease of the central nervous system. Degeneration of this system and sensation of touch affects other parts of the body, including the muscles so necessary for locomotion. I have not moved from a cane ten years ago to a wheelchair today without frustrations. As a wife, a mother, one who sorts the laundry while sitting on the kitchen floor, who is dependent upon my son to vacuum the rug, who must lean heavily in many ways upon my husband, I have problems. It is not easy always to be on the receiving end of things. I have my periods of depression. But then God through one of His children comes along and lifts my feet from the miry clay and places them upon a rock. How I praise God for my comforters. It is the title of one of my books, *My Comforters.* Let me give you one illustration of how God used a sister in the church to raise me from the sloughs of despair.

Recently I was in one of those periods of depression. I knew it, my family knew it, my parents who were visiting us knew it. I was feeling sorry for myself. I felt I was a burden. I wanted people to lean on me instead of me needing to lean on them. With my illness the summer heat completely incapacitates me. Air conditioning is a must in both the house and car. We had just had the expense of installing air conditioning in the car—an expense we could ill afford. It was necessary because of me. Perhaps that knowledge added to the depression I was already experiencing.

Then a letter came from a woman in Ohio. She mentioned that while waiting for her husband to complete a committee meeting at church, she picked up my book, *My Comforters,* and read again from it. She wanted to come and help me with my housework, but could not. So she was sending me a check to help instead. My vision was already somewhat impaired at the time, but I could tell by the decimal that it was not a check for five dollars, or for fifty dollars. It was almost the exact sum of our air conditioning expense, an expense of which she had no knowledge. I turned to my family, to my parents, people who were coping so graciously with me as I was down, and said, "Oh, how do I deserve this?" And I knew I did not, yet God lifted me again through one of my comforters.

Why doesn't God heal me? Can He not do it? Oh, yes, He can. He healed our baby, Becky, when she had severe diarrhea and became desperately dehydrated, when we were ready to take her to the hospital for intravenous feeding. At a church service in Iowa City, a lay person in an informal, spontaneous manner led the congregation in prayer for her recovery. And from that very hour she began to improve. God healed her. I know God is able to heal me.

Do I stay in my wheelchair because of lack of faith? This is one of the great trials of my affliction, when well meaning friends suggest that lack of faith on the part of my husband, Virgil, and I is the obstruction that blocks my healing. Letters and telephone calls, personal visits from friends like those of Job, gently or harshly suggest (even insist) that miserly faith on our part stops God from doing this work of grace in my life. It seems so strange to us to hear that accusation when we know that He is even now working a work of grace in my life. Yes, it is a burden we bear. I have told God that He can heal me any time He chooses. My faith is in Him.

God has said, not just to Paul, but to me personally, "My grace is sufficient for thee." I believe that many faith healers lack a theology of suffering. They do not seem to understand that many people accomplish things in spite of problems, that problems are catalysts. I am listening just now to a talking book for the blind, a record of John Milton's "Paradise Lost." He wrote it when he was blind. He wrote it in spite of his blindness. Would this epic work have come forth without his blindness?

I personally wonder if instant healing in my case would help everyone concerned. It might make it difficult for some with whom I now have good rapport. Certain blessings come from speaking engagements extended to me because of my handicap. I do not speak to them of pity. I speak of understanding. And this would be lost, if I were healed. If this is the reason why God does not heal me, I accept it. To be understood can be better than to be healed.

I cannot analyze God's thinking toward me, place Him in a box, limit His program for my life. I cannot say that He has chosen me from among many to suffer with multiple sclerosis. I would say that it is equally normal for God to heal and not to heal. When we as finite beings attempt to analyze the Infinite Being, we are in trouble. It is enough to know that God loves, that God provides.

If people wish to pray for me, praying for one splashy healing, it is all right. I am in God's hands. I am a bit more inclined at present, however, to ask people to pray for enabling grace for me, grace in small doses. I believe that when God wants you to do something, He will enable you to do it. I am working just now on two different books at the same time. And God is providing the grace I need each day.

Physical healing is a bit like spiritual healing. We live in hope. As Christians we cannot insist on heaven now. We still struggle against sin on this earth. In heaven it will be different. There will be no sin in that place to struggle against. Nor will there be wheelchairs in heaven.

Paul wrote in bonds. And so do I. As I inferred, I believe that every person on this earth lives in spite of something. I live in spite of multiple sclerosis. I live as a privileged handicapped person. I live, I exist because of God's love, my husband's love, my children's love, the love of my church, the love of my many comforters everywhere. It is a good place to be, in the center of God's love, surrounded by His comforters, my comforters.

5 THIS CHILD SHOULD HAVE DIED

● Marilyn Denlinger

I WANT to tell you about the healing of our young daughter, Charity. Her name means love. And, like all parents, Ray and I love this child. God gave her to us twice, once when she was born, and once when He healed her. I want to tell about her healing for God's honor and glory. He gave her back to us, and we want her to be used by Him.

On June 11, 1972, our seven-year-old daughter had what I called at the time simply a "bug bite." I brushed from her hair what I thought was an insect, one that she complained had bitten her. Later I found out that it was not a true insect. We found out a lot of things in the next few days, but especially that God hears the

Marilyn Denlinger is a nurse; her husband, Ray, a successful real estate investor, entered seminary in 1973 to prepare himself for a new career as a pastor. They have one other child, a son, Scott. The family lives at Harrisonburg, Virginia during the school year and Lancaster, Pennsylvania in the summer where they care for 80 apartments which are a part of their present business.

prayer of His people. How the joy wells up in my heart as I think back over those weeks. As parents we were subjected to great distress, much worry, great concern. But we found a pearl of great price. We were richly rewarded. We found that God cares for us.

On June 13, Charity complained of headaches and began running a fever. I called our family physician. Since there was flu around, he said to force fluids and give aspirin. That night she began vomiting and I took her to the doctor the next day, Wednesday. At that time the doctor thought Charity's trouble was due to a hyper-systemic reaction to a bee sting, perhaps unrelated to the "bug" which I had brushed from her hair.

Another day went by, June 15, and our daughter's condition worsened. We kept in contact with the doctor and various medications were tried. But there was no improvement.

By Saturday night Charity was covered with an itchy rash which we had first noticed in very slight form on Wednesday. Our family physician was out of town, so we saw another general practitioner. His diagnosis was the same, but he ordered new medication.

Monday night there was no improvement. Charity had weakened to the extent that it was necessary to carry her to the bathroom. Tuesday morning our doctor was back in town and upon seeing her, ordered her straight to the hospital.

There we were referred to a pediatrician who after many questions gave a new diagnosis of Rocky Mountain Spotted Fever. The "bug" that we thought had bitten her was an infected tick. This was now the tenth day after the tick bite, and even though there was a specific medicine for this disease, they could not be sure that its administration would be in time. And they warned that the medication was only 50% of the battle. The ability, the willingness of our daughter to fight back, would hold the balance of power. But by the time of her admission to the hospital she had become lethargic, sometimes irrational, and incoherent. We were frightened parents. Charity was so weak, her condition had so deteriorated, that we wondered if she could fight back.

On Wednesday morning she went into a coma with right side paralysis, with spastic right arm and foot. Her pupils were fixed. Our pediatrician started I.V.'s and had an electrocardiogram done because of a noticeable heart murmur. A neurologist was called in because of possible brain damage. Her spleen was enlarged. Lots of blood work was being done. I thank God for men and women who have chosen the healing arts as their career. God used them.

That evening, Wednesday, June 21, my husband began calling relatives and friends. We wanted the prayers of God's people. A friend in Virginia who feels that he has the gift of laying on hands for healing heard about our request for prayer and offered to come to the hospital and minister to our daughter. Ray said, "No, we have faith to believe that God will heal her regardless of where people are as they pray." We did not want any one person's act to come into focus as being responsible for Charity's healing. If Charity was to be healed, we wanted God to have the glory.

After we knew that so many were praying, Ray and I had a real calmness within, a peace, and willingness to accept the death of Charity if God so chose at that time. Even Charity seemed to relax and was less spastic.

By Thursday afternooon, she seemed to notice me, although she did not respond. Our pediatrician and neurologist reassured us that she had passed the crisis, that she might recover. One doctor said, "Keep hoping and praying." We testified that we were, and he said, "I know you are."

In a couple of more days, our daughter started saying

a few words and was able to begin eating and drinking again. She had been in the hospital for ten days.

My husband and I feel that this was one of God's gradual healings. Nothing happened instantaneously. Charity did not leap from her bed healed. God works in different ways to perform His wonders. But we are as certain that God healed her as Jairus was in the story found in Matthew 9:18-26. God does not always heal in a twinkling of the eye. He can, but sometimes He chooses otherwise. Why? I don't know. Perhaps in heaven I will ask Him, but again, perhaps I won't. There will probably be more beautiful things to talk about up there.

A final check by the physician in her case said the healing was complete. We believe him, because we believe God. Our neurologist said, "According to all statistics, having been so ill, this child should have died." Again, we believe, but God's laws defy statistical analysis.

We are grateful for all that the medical profession did for Charity in this time of crisis. We thank them for it. And we are grateful to God for what He did for her in this time of crisis also. We thank Him too.

Witnesses:
> Ruth Denlinger
> Route 1
> Ronks, Pennsylvania 17572
>
> Joan Martin
> Route 6
> Harrisonburg, Virginia 22801

6 TWICE ANOINTED, TWICE HEALED

● Ella May Miller

Twice I was anointed with oil for my healing. Once it was in the Chaco of Argentina, South America. The second time it was at the Mt. Clinton Mennonite Church of Virginia, U.S.A. In South America a Toba Indian preacher assisted my husband in the anointing service. In the United States my husband assisted Chester K. Lehman and Mahlon Blosser. In South America I was near death and God healed me. In North America the physicians said I must submit to surgery for my healing. God said, "I can do it without surgery." And He did.

I am afraid that the above paragraph is misleading. I must do some confessing. In the past I have not always

Ella May Miller, pastor's wife, mother of four, former missionary to South America, is best known as the voice of Heart to Heart, a women's radio program originating in Harrisonburg, Virginia. She is a writer and frequent speaker at family conferences, before civic groups, and at women's retreats.

felt comfortable in discussing divine healing. In fact, I remember little teaching about this ordinance in our church. And yet it is clearly stated in the Bible.

I saw it only as a device that some could use, hoping to escape pain, medication, surgery. I did not see it as an avenue upon which I would travel, a street upon which I would meet God in a fuller, finer way. I believed that there was such a thing as divine healing, but I ruled it out for myself.

And now I am giving my testimony about God's miraculous healing in my life. Twice I met God afresh through this beautiful ordinance as practiced in the brotherhood of believers. Now I am giving Him the glory for that which I once ignored, rejected, spurned. I believe in divine healing.

God has been speaking to me in this area for many years. And I have not been a good listener. God has been teaching me, and I have not been a good pupil. God has been ministering to me, and I have not always been receptive to that ministering. But God was patient with me, like He is with all His children. I praise Him for new light, new understanding, new assurance in this area.

Why did I not see this earlier? I don't know. Surely God has been speaking to me for many years. I remember when He came through to me so clearly in Argentina. I opened my eyes for the moment, then nearly shut them again.

My husband and I were serving as missionaries in South America. We were somewhat isolated in a frontier community of the Chaco in northern Argentina. It would have been a good time for me to lean heavily upon God. I chose instead to argue with Him.

On April 23, 1951, I gave birth to our fourth child, a little girl, Jeanne. I was in a small hospital clinic run by a Hungarian refugee doctor in the town of Saenz Pena. He was fully competent, and I needed all his skills.

About a week after I delivered, I developed a thrombosis condition that led me to the point of death. In fact, the symptoms of death were there. My tongue was thick, my hands waxen and cold, my fingernails cyanotic.

And in my pain and delirium, I remember chastising God, telling Him what He had to do because of what we had already done for Him. Had we not come as missionaries to South America? "God, You can't let this happen to me," I insisted. "You owe life to me."

I thought of my husband, Sam, left with our four children, one new born. I thought of our yielding to that Macedonian call, "Come over into the Chaco and help us." And now God was going to let me die. He didn't dare.

I know now that this was wretched thinking, but on what seemed to be my deathbed, those were the rebellious thoughts flooding my mind. I did not gently ask God for healing. I demanded life of Him. It was my right.

But on that bed God began to remold my mind. A verse from the Bible came sifting into my clouded thinking. It was that verse Jesus spoke in John 6:38 where He says, "For I came down from heaven, not to do my own will, but the will of Him that sent me." And I wondered whose will I wanted done in the Chaco: God's will or Ella May Miller's will?

Thoughts of shame replaced the rebellious ones. God moved me to the place where I was pliable, where I could say, "Okay, Lord. Your will, not mine." It was a spiritual crisis as well as a physical crisis.

There was no instantaneous healing of my body after that decision. Yet I heard God clearly saying to me, "Ella May, you are going to live." And I began to mend.

But God still had things to teach me about His healing works. A week after my thinking became straightened out, my left leg was swollen to twice its normal size. Phlebitis had developed.

During all of my vacillating, my husband had a far better, more consistent approach to God than that which I have described about myself.

It was a terrible strain on him, caring for our three older children, ministering to the Indians on the mission field, traveling the eighteen miles each day to be with me. But he functioned well, he thought clearly. And when my leg became inflamed, he suggested an anointing.

One day he brought with him a Toba Indian, Carlos Rodriguez. He was a minister among those we served. They planned to ask God in a special way for my healing. They would not demand it like I had, but they would seek it by the biblical method of anointing with oil. And so they did.

The phlebitic condition remained with me for two and one-half months. It took me almost two years before I could walk aright. And even then, it was with pain.

I suppose some would question if that is really divine healing. Couldn't God do better than that, speed things up, straighten things out in the twinkling of an eye?

Of course, He could have done so. But I have learned that God is sovereign. To realize that fact, to accept it, means that Romans 8:28 of the Bible becomes viable in my life. Believe me, I did not learn it overnight. Like I said, I have been a slow learner in God's school of wisdom.

The years from 1941 to 1953 were years of changing opinion for me. It became necessary for us to leave the mission field, to return to the United States. Those years became years of growth, of God gently, graciously

changing my opinion. It was a period of Him strength-
ening and healing me emotionally as well as spiritually.

As a former missionary, as the wife of a pastor in
the Mennonite Church, as present speaker on the na-
tional *Heart to Heart* radio broadcast, you might think
that I would be above such things, that I would always
be on top of everything. It is not so. All of us, regardless
of our position or accomplishments, need God's touch-
ing, guiding, shaping, correcting hand. I praise God too
that I have also felt His healing hand.

I remarked at the beginning about the healing service
at the Mt. Clinton church in Virginia that is pastored
at present by my husband. And even in this, God was
still changing me. I hope He never stops doing so.

For several years I had suffered from a slow but
constant hemorrhaging from my body. Surgery had been
suggested as a possible cure. I felt that God was directing
me to seek healing through an anointing service. In
South America, during that deep illness, I had little to
say about that lovely incident. Now, I could think clearly
about it. So, I said to God, "Yes, Lord, I am ready
to have an anointing service for this problem. But let
it be in the privacy of my home."

And God came back with, "No, it should be in the
church. You are able to walk. There is no reason why
it should not be shared with the fellowship at the Mt.
Clinton Church."

I shuddered at the public display.

Yet, I knew in my heart that it was God's will. And
I remembered my Chaco verse, how Christ came to do
the will of His Father. And I decided to do His will
also.

It would be dramatic in a testimony like this to tell
you how I felt a "light from heaven" effect the moment
God healed me at that little church on that summer

Sunday, July 5, 1964. Then I would have been like the woman who touched the hem of Jesus' garment in Matthew 9:20.

But it was different with me that day. I felt His blessed presence. I rested my ailment with Him. In that sense I knew that I had touched the hem of His garment. I felt that He touched me.

Within a year the issue of blood ceased. And I knew my healing was complete. I praise God afresh for that healing. I have learned to bring each ache, each pain, each sickness to Him. The devil often comes to me, and I rebuke him each time by referring to that act of faith on July 5, 1964.

God does not always heal in the same manner and within certain time limits. I have learned not to make my experience a philosophy, to present it as God's pattern for everyone. I present it only as the way He dealt with me. I think it is wonderful that God ministers to each of us so fully, so perfectly, so understandingly, supplying us each with just what we need for that particular time.

I am so thankful for a personal God, one who sees me as a single sheep in His vast flock. And on me He poured His healing love. I could ask no more for myself.

I could ask no more for you.

Witnesses:

> Mahlon L. Bosser
> Route 5, Box 86
> Harrisonburg, Virginia 22801
>
> Chester K. Lehman
> 1033 College Avenue
> Harrisonburg, Virginia 22801

7 FROM HOSPITAL BED TO PULPIT

● Nelson R. Roth

ON MARCH 1, 1951, I celebrated my eleventh birthday in the hospital. The nurses on the children's ward gave me a party. Everyone assumed that it would be my last birthday. Today, some twenty years later, I am a minister of the gospel. God healed me. At my healing I made a special commitment of myself to God, and both of us took that commitment seriously. He called me to serve Him as a pastor.

Our church stationery has this verse printed on it: "We preach not ourselves, but Christ Jesus the Lord; and ourselves your servants for Jesus' sake" (2 Corinthians 4:5). That's what I want my testimony to be, a testimony that will direct the reader's attention to God, not to Nelson R. Roth.

My story begins when I was nine years old. In Febru-

Nelson R. Roth pastors the Martinsburg Mennonite Church in Martinsburg, Pennsylvania. He is married, has three sons and one daughter, and teaches in the public schools.

ary, 1950, I was hospitalized for ten days with an attack of rheumatic fever. I was discharged from the hospital on my tenth birthday, but I returned one week later for another stay of four weeks. From April through September of that year I was confined in bed with absolutely no physical exercise or exertion permitted due to an enlarged heart and severe heart murmur. In rheumatic fever there is the frequent danger of heart damage. My heart was damaged.

Can you imagine what it is like for a boy of ten to lie in bed for six months? They were long and painful months. Through the window I watched the ending of spring, the passage of summer, the beginning of fall. And I wondered about life and why I had to be sick. I wondered why God selected me to be a prisoner in a bed. My father, Paul, was a minister and that made me a P.K., a preacher's kid. Lots of things are said about preacher's kids. They often live a tough life, but I thought God was really pouring it on when He allowed this to happen to me. When your friends are playing ball, driving tractors, visiting, all while you lie in bed, it's hard to be happy. It's easier to turn your head to the wall like that king did in the Bible and ask God a little one word question, "Why?"

I couldn't go to school that fall and for a time I had homebound instruction. That's when a teacher comes right to your home and gives you your lessons. But I got up tight about everything, and had to stop it. Can a fellow of ten have a nervous breakdown? I don't know.

But I do know this, that in February of 1951, I had to go back to the hospital again, and that was worse than lying at home and asking God, "Why?" For six weeks I got penicillin shots every three hours around the clock. And there was no improvement. I felt like I was a pin cushion. The joints in my legs, arms, and neck were swollen and painful. My heart continued to be affected. And my condition got critical. That's when my birthday party came. I was eleven on March 1, 1951. I guess everybody thought it was going to be my last one. I wasn't sure. When a person is around ten or eleven, he may daydream about dying, but that's about all. And it's a lot safer. You feel a little different about it when you know you're not well, when you think you might be pretty sick.

I got no better. That Easter, other patients were getting Easter baskets and cards. My diet had been restricted, but my pediatrician, realizing that my hopes were slim, gave ward orders that I could eat whatever I wanted. My appetite for chocolate candy was rewarded as I took advantage of the generosity of the other patients. I'm sure the hospital personnel did not realize how I enjoyed such an opportunity.

It was fun to eat what I wanted, and actually I felt better for a little while. Then I began to get severe nose bleeds, and one night I had an emergency transfusion of two pints of blood.

I can recall clearly the excitement of the doctor and the nurses as they frantically worked with me that night. I was growing weaker and everything beyond the foot of my bed became hazy. I felt as though a cloud was surrounding me. Death? Maybe. God's presence? I believed He was there.

Due to the extensive loss of blood my veins had collapsed and the doctor was frantically trying, without success, to locate a vein which would receive the transfusion. After the doctor made repeated and painful attempts for prominent veins on the tops of my hands and feet, I heard one of the nurses announce that my blood pressure had dropped extremely low and that my heart was irregular. In desperation the doctor turned

to me and said, "Pray, Nelson, pray!" God answered
that prayer and almost immediately the new blood
began to enter my body.

I got through that crisis, but my general condition
worsened. Finally they thought that they had done all
they could for me at the Uniontown Hospital where
I remained weak, yet still struggling for life. My parents
could not afford to have me transferred to a more
specialized hospital where I could get more intensive
treatment. But my doctor arranged for me to be admitted
to the Pittsburgh Children's Hospital free of charge as
a research patient. I guess I was going to be sort of
a guinea pig. But I never made that transfer.

My father was pastor of the Masontown Mennonite
Church and he talked to me about divine healing and
anointing with oil. I had become a Christian before I
first got sick and was baptized at home in bed during
my first illness. I knew what it was to be a Christian,
and when Pop explained about divine healing, I said
I was ready.

Our bishop, A. J. Metzler, from Scottsdale, Pennsylvania, anointed me with oil at the hospital, and prayed
for my healing. It was on Wednesday evening at the
same time that our church was having their regular
weekly prayer meeting. My parents, of course, were there
at the hospital on that special night when I was anointed
for my healing.

There was no light from heaven, no noticeable change
that night, but God must have set the healing process
in order. When my parents came back the next day
to see me, I was sitting up in bed, the first time in
six weeks. Even my parents were hardly prepared for
that. Sometimes God takes a grain of mustard seed faith
and makes a tree out of it.

One and a half weeks later, on a Sunday morning,

I was discharged from the hospital and returned home with instructions to restrict my activities. I was not, however, required to be bedfast as during the previous spring and summer. And that was really wonderful.

And it has been wonderful to sit here and recall what God did for me as a boy of eleven. I've tried to share my thoughts with you as I recall them. It's hard to remember everything. You see, now it's more than twenty years later. I have not had a relapse, nor have I been a patient in the hospital for any other reason. The doctors said I would never be able to do any strenuous work, but since than I have been fully active with no physical limitations.

I returned to the out-patient heart clinic for six years for an annual checkup. Each time the heart specialist marveled at the continual progress I had made, for it far surpassed what he expected. It doesn't surprise me. As a minister of the gospel for nine years, I have learned to expect big things from God.

Through the difficult time of illness and recovery God had much for me to learn. From my parents I witnessed patience, understanding, tolerance, and spiritual endurance. Through the generosity of friends near and far who knew my father and learned of my condition and circumstances, I came to realize the joy of those who shared in Christian brotherhood. Having received so much from God through other people, I have since been committed to discovering the greater joy of giving so that others may receive. God has blessed our family materially, as well as physically and spiritually. In gratitude to Him for this, my wife and I, during the first ten years of our marriage have endeavored to increase our financial giving to the Lord's work. Even though we are not wealthy and our income is average, we have now passed our third tithe (30%) and we continue to believe that God wants to bless our stewardship of money as well as the stewardship of our time and abilities—all for His glory.

I don't know why God doesn't heal every child with rheumatic fever. But I know that He healed me. I will praise Him for it through all of eternity.

Witnesses:

       Paul M. Roth
       202 Old 33
       Harrisonburg, Virginia 22801

       A. J. Metzler
       Route 5, Box 145
       Mt. Pleasant, Pennsylvania 15666

8 WE PRAYED FOR OUR SON— AND HE LIVED

● Linda Heatwole

LIKE all proud parents, we have many photos of our
first child. The one I treasure most was taken in Algeria,
North Africa. It is a simple black and white, a bit
underexposed. At the time it was snapped our son was
only two months old. We have more recent pictures,
finely posed, in lovely color. But this one is precious.

Every time I look at that picture, my heart sings out
in praise to God. That tiny child in my arms looks so
weak, so helpless, so innocent. I remember when his
death seemed only an hour or so away, when three fine
physicians had exhausted their skills upon him. Then
God took over, and our son lived. My husband and
I like to testify of that beautiful experience.

Linda and her husband, Dr. Stanley Heatwole, live in Staunton,
Virginia, where he has his medical practice. They are associate members of the Covenant Presbyterian Church. Boulaid Larken, Algerian
by birth, whose healing they report, is their adopted son. They also
have a daughter, Malika Renee. The Heatwoles are actively involved
with international friends and students in their community.

It's interesting. Some years ago a new message was being heard in the world. The message was, "God is dead." My husband, Stanley, and I have never fallen into such a depressing, blasphemous, theological void. God is real to us, very real. We know that God cares, that He lives in our hearts through the presence of His Son, Jesus Christ. When I look at that picture, when I remember the prayer miracle that occurred, I know God is alive. We talked to Him then; we talk to Him now.

On Christmas Day we commemorate the coming of Jesus into this world. Boulaid Larkem came to us also on Christmas Day—and he came wrapped in swaddling clothes, a custom of the Near East. A little child who was present that day exclaimed, "He's just like the Baby Jesus!" We thought so too.

Our experience with divine healing is a bit involved. During 1968-1972, Stan and I were serving under the Mennonite Central Committee in Algeria, North Africa. Stan had graduated from medical school and we wanted to give several years of our lives in Christian service in a needy land. We volunteered for such service and were sent to the former French colony of Algeria. It is a land of Arabs, a land of the Moslem religion, a land where many people are very poor.

On Christmas Day in 1968 our son arrived. He was ten days old. Of course, he was not our natural son, and at that time we had no idea that he would ever become our son by adoption.

Born of Algerian parents, Boulaid Larkem came to our little mission home through a set of sad circumstances. His mother died shortly after childbirth and his father was not able to care for him. We accepted the responsibility of caring for him temporarily.

Then we fell in love with Boulaid. (Today, he is our adopted son. And for us to legally bring him from

Algeria to the States, to be able to adopt him as our son, was also somewhat of a miracle. But that is the God we worship, a God of miracles.)

In February the child became ill. We had cared for him through January and this was his second month with us. The illness came about suddenly. It was a severe case of diarrhea and dehydration. A more official diagnosis by the three physicians of our small clinic was gastroenteritis. An inflammation of his digestive tract seemed to initiate the troubles. There may have been other medical problems, but it was impossible to diagnose more accurately than that. Our laboratory facilities were very limited where we were stationed. At that time intravenous solutions were not available there. And for dehydration cases such as Boulaid's, I.V.'s are essential to replace the body fluids that are so rapidly lost.

Twenty-four hours after our child became ill, it was no longer a question of "Will he die?" but rather, "When will he die?" The three American physicians did medically all they could for the infant. And yet all symptoms indicated that death was only a few hours away.

Can you imagine the helpless, hopeless feeling we had? We had the help of three highly trained medical doctors, men who had spent eight years beyond high school in training to diagnose, treat, and heal. But there in North Africa we felt so keenly man's own inadequacies to maintain life. And Boulaid's life was slipping away before our eyes.

I sat on the bed holding the dying child. His respiration was so faint that I had to raise his tiny nightgown to see if he was actually breathing. Boulaid had now been with us six weeks, and we loved him. We did not want to see him die. But the doctors had done all that they could humanly do. And thus the stage was set to call upon the Great Physician.

As I held that child I wanted so desperately to live,

the Holy Spirit led me to ask Dr. John Keiser, who was hovering nearby, to pray for Boulaid's healing.

Some doctors find it difficult to turn from trusting in their medical training and ask for help from another source that goes beyond the skills acquired in medical school, internship, and residency. But a Christian doctor has a different perspective. And Dr. John Keiser is a Christian doctor. He bowed his head and led us in prayer for Boulaid who seemed so close to death.

It was a simple prayer, not couched in medical terms. He prayed quietly for the healing of this little Arab child. And as he led us in prayer our hearts were filled with a mixture of love and hope and trust.

Within an hour improvement came. There was no good medical explanation for it. In the prayer Dr. Keiser had mentioned our desire for God's will to be done. The improvement was God's answer, giving us a specific sign, a hope we scarcely dared ask for.

The change was dramatic. Boulaid began to breathe easier. I could now see his breathing efforts through his nightgown. His pupils began to respond to light. And above all, he cried when his diaper was changed. He had always done that when he was healthy, but since his sickness he had lain there impassively, too weak to cry. But now he cried, and it was music to our ears. Parents usually do not like to hear their children cry, but we rejoiced in those cries of protest. Truly, God went beyond man's ability to heal.

Boulaid was not out of danger yet, for he went into shock on two separate occasions during the month of February. But God was faithful and each time he responded to medical treatment.

At this writing Boulaid is a healthy boy of four. He is normal in every way and shows no residual effects from his illness.

In Algeria adoption is impossible, even among Algerians. But we had faith that if this baby was meant to live, he was also meant to be our child. We were allowed to take him out of the country, and in 1972, he became our child by adoption. We felt that he was ours before, but now it was legalized.

It's a bit like entering God's family. Christ is always available, and God longs to make us heirs and joint heirs with Him. Already we have been purchased; we belong to God. But membership in God's family becomes official, legal, only when we completely open our hearts to the Son of God and let Him take full possession of us. Then the "papers are signed" and we know we belong to Him.

We have many pictures of our son, but I love most to look at that one of myself holding Boulaid when he was just a few weeks old. I remember many hours I spent rocking him in that little, crowded Algerian bedroom.

In that photograph Boulaid is looking up, his eyes attracted to something above. He is not smiling; he looks sad, worried. He is only two months old, a bit young to be worried. I picture him talking to God, perhaps saying, "Lord, I'm just a little Arab boy. My mother has died. My father cannot care for me. Now these people have me. What will happen to me?"

And the God I know is answering him, "My child, I care for every sparrow that falls. I care for you. You came to this house on Christmas Day. I sent My own Son into the world on such a day. Some received Him; some did not. Your new parents have received you. I have placed you in a home where you will learn of Me, where you will receive My Son as your Savior."

Is that what my son was thinking? Is that what God said back to him? A mother has a right to think such things, to believe such things.

In my life, in the life of my husband, God is not

dead. We have only to look at that picture and we are reminded of His reality, His love, His involvement with us.

We have written of our experience because we wanted to share it with as many people as possible.

We believe in praising God for what He has done in our lives, for healing our son, Boulaid.

Witnesses:

> Dr. and Mrs. John Keiser, M.D.
> 311 Orchard Drive
> Cedar Falls, Iowa 50613

> Dr. Stanley Heatwole, M.D.
> 120 Sproul Lane
> Staunton, Virginia 24401

9 WE PRAYED FOR OUR SON— AND HE DIED

● Ora M. and Grace Yoder

WHEN OUR SON, Leon Yoder, went to Indonesia, we were both concerned and pleased. Parents like to have their children close to them. Indonesia was half way around the world. And we were concerned.

But he had chosen in lieu of service in the military to spend several years in Pax, an organization dedicated to peacefully serving our fellowmen. And so we were pleased.

Leon went to the Indonesian island of Java just three months after his graduation from Goshen College, Goshen, Indiana. He left in September, 1963, to serve as an administrative assistant under Mennonite Central Committee (MCC). His training at Goshen in business and economics enabled him to shoulder immediately the finance and shipping affairs of the MCC work in

_____

Ora and Grace Yoder live just outside the quiet village of Shipshewana in northern Indiana. Their residence on State Road 5 is near the department store Mr. Yoder has operated for many years.

the islands. God gave him the insight and the ability to work at lowering the racial barriers between youth of Chinese and Javanese descent, a situation comparable to the black-white problem in the United States.

Our son had a small mole on his shoulder blade. It became irritated through his frequent driving in connection with his work. It was surgically removed. Leon wrote to us, describing the incident in his quiet way with humor: "The growth turned out to be the size of a grapefruit. . . ." Then he added the word, "seed," to describe it more accurately. And we smiled. It was like Leon. And we feared not.

This was in the middle of December, his second Christmas month in the islands. It should have been a joyful period both for our son and us as his parents. But by Christmas it was a different story. He wrote of being weak and run down, and that he needed to stay in bed part of the time. And we feared.

And then a lump appeared under his right arm. In Indonesia there was concern; in Shipshewana, Indiana, there was concern. We were kept informed.

A tissue sample was sent to Hong Kong to check for possible malignancy. But our son's condition worsened and it was decided not to wait for the report. Leon would be flown to the United States to enter the Evanston Hospital, Chicago, Illinois for extensive testing and treatment.

His return home, alone, was one of mixed pain, rejoicing, sadness, and consciousness of God's divine leading. God intervened at once so that the government processing of papers that was necessary for his departure were speeded through in a matter of days instead of weeks.

The airport he would leave from was at Djakarta. He traveled there by rail. At an intermediate stop he was taken off the train by police who feared that his sickness was contagious. But as Leon waited in the railroad depot, wondering how God would solve this problem, a physician whom he knew, "happened" to come into that depot. It was God at work, intervening again. The physician was able to persuade the officials to allow our son to continue his trip. It seems God wanted our son to return to us for the last few weeks of his life.

In Hawaii there were problems with custom agents. They told Leon to leave the plane and pass through the regular customs check in the terminal building. Our son was under sedation and very weak. He did not feel strong enough to leave the plane. The custom agent insisted. A stewardess insisted in stronger language that the inspection would have to be on the plane. And it was.

Although Leon was to be awakened every four hours on the long flight for medication, this was not always done. In San Francisco and Chicago there were delays and misunderstandings.

The worst experience was in Chicago. Because of failure to consider the International Dateline in time calculations, our son arrived twenty-four hours before we expected to meet him. Hurried calls from the O'Hare International Airport sent us speeding to his side. And then we knew he was where the best of medical skills would be available. Dr. Willard Krabill, our family physician at Goshen, had made all the necessary arrangements for our son to be admitted to the hospital at Evanston. He and all the medical staff we encountered were most helpful. And we prayed. Oh, how we prayed!

Upon the advice of those examining Leon, radical surgery was proposed. It was thought best to remove the right arm, much of the right shoulder. Leon consented; we consented.

Just prior to the amputation the doctors did some exploratory surgery to check the liver. They found that the melanoma cancer had gone too far. Surgery would not save our son. Leon's recovery through medical help would now rest in chemotherapy, the injection of experimental drugs.

But we believed in divine healing, that God could work and minister in our son's healing. We never forgot God. We knew it would take a miracle, but our God is a God of miracles. And so we prayed.

After twelve days at Evanston, Leon was moved by ambulance under the constant care of Dr. Krabill to the Goshen Hospital where the treatment was continued.

Each night we had our devotions about Leon's bed. Often Pastor Bob Detweiler of the College congregation and long time friend of our son, along with Dr. Willard Krabill were with us. And we joined hands and hearts in praying for the one so ill.

Other prayers arose from many, many places. From Goshen College, from the Mennonite Board of Missions, from the Shore Mennonite Church where Leon held his membership, from friends in surrounding states, from almost countless people.

And on April 5, 1965, the son for whose healing we prayed, died.

As we look back, over the intervening years, we cannot help but feel sorrow. Our son was important to us, beloved and honored. To say that his living did not matter to us would be false. We wanted Leon to live, wanted desperately for him to live. And we prayed with faith for his recovery. And he died.

Now how do we feel about this whole matter of divine healing, of prayer, of God's will, of our own desires? for surely they are inseparably linked.

Perhaps our son, as he lay dying in the hospital, quite

conscious that he was dying, expressed it best for all of us. He said, "This is not the way we would have planned it. But if this is the way God wants it, then it is better than any plan we might devise." And as his parents, we must agree.

When our son was still in Indonesia, S. Djojohardjo, the brilliant, charismatic head of the Indonesian Mennonite Church, a man to whom God has given the gift of healing, was asked to pray for our son.

He struggled to do so, but could not. The Spirit would not let him. He could only pray, "Let God be glorified in this illness."

His prayer was a prophecy that is coming true. In the hospitals, at Goshen College, in our community, in our family, God has brought about a work of healing, of peace, of consecration, of changed lives, of amazement at God's ministry through suffering and death.

Leon said before he died, "If this suffering of mine makes some young person rethink his life, it's worthwhile." From the personal testimony of at least one local pastor we know this has happened.

Our son's last audible prayer was for the church in Indonesia.

Few people knew that while Leon was in Indonesia, he arranged to provide a scholarship to an Indonesian friend to enable him to get his Master's Degree at a Christian university.

As Leon's parents we have set up an endowment fund at Goshen College in memory of our son, Leon C. Yoder. It will perpetuate the memory of his personal values and deep devotion to Christ. Indonesian students will have priority for the annual income from the memorial endowment because of our son's intense interest in his Mennonite Central Committee's assignment in Indonesia.

Following is a letter written to Leon just a few days before his death. We sought healing for our son, and found healing for ourselves. Even in Leon's death we praise God.

Dear Leon:

"The heavens declare the glory of God; and the firmament sheweth his handiwork. Day unto day uttereth speech, and night unto night sheweth knowledge. There is no speech nor language, where their voice is not heard. Their line is gone out through all the earth, and the words to the end of the world."

Hundreds of Christians are holding you up to the throne of grace, and are not able to understand why this is happening.

You are able to see the beautiful handiwork of God in so many places and in so many different ways—especially in flowers. I must often think of the lovely design and color combinations of that one flower, whose beauty you caught in that one picture. It was in its prime.

Now it seems that God wants a bouquet of flowers in their prime for a special occasion and would like for you to fill that one special place. Would to God, He would have selected me, but my petals are about ready to fall, and the most beautiful and useful years are about past.

I, as a father, appreciate the inspiration you have been to me and the many lessons I have learned from your life, your reliance upon God and His wisdom, your appreciation of God's handiwork as shown in nature, in trees, in mountains, water, sky, and in the songs of birds and insects.

And, above all, your appreciation of the beauty and revelations of God as you found them in flowers and nature, your interest in the kingdom and your enthusiasm for the things of God make a father happy that God has seen wise to let you live among us for these few years.

I am looking forward to the time I can see you across on that other shore.

"The Lord gave, and the Lord hath taken away; blessed be the name of the Lord."

With love,
Dad

EDITOR'S NOTE
After the above chapter was written, we received this note from the Millers: "We also had a daughter, Elaine, who was ill with diabetes in a Chicago hospital when Robert Baker interviewed us for Leon's story. She passed away on January 7, 1974. We know that she too is in heaven according to her testimony before she died. Of course we also loved her and prayed for her."

10 THE "MOTH EATEN" ILLIUM

● Robert Witmer

I WAS FORTY YEARS OLD when I met plasma cell cytoma, cancer of the bone. I saw the diagnosis written in red ink on the doctor's notes in the famed Curie Hospital in Paris, France, a hospital that is devoted to cancer research and treatment.

The day I learned the true nature of my ailment was a long one. And that night was not a good time for sleeping. My wife, Lois, and I lay awake much of the night, darkness without, swirling questions within. We crossed many bridges as we lay there, bridges that we had not actually come to. But in those first desperate hours our minds flew into the future, refused to lie dormant, to be static. We had fears. With five children, ages four to nineteen, a cancer diagnosis gnawing away at me physically and at my wife and I emotionally, fears

---

Robert Witmer, a native of Ontario, Canada, has served near Paris, France, as a missionary for the past seventeen years. He and his wife, Lois, are the parents of five children.

come easily. Near dawn we committed everything to the Lord. The previous Sunday I had preached a sermon to our small congregation of some fifty persons at Chatenay-Malabry, France, a village just outside of Paris. The sermon title was, "God Is Here." I had little thought that we would need to draw so deeply upon the substance of the sermon that very week. But I did. It turned out to be one of those special messages from God, more needed by me than anyone in the congregation.

The initial pain on that first Sunday in October, 1969, announced itself as I found it necessary to change a tire on one of the buses that would be used early the next morning to pick up the retarded children for the school and workshop that our congregation had initiated, a work that had prospered and was now being supported by the French Government. In the process of bending over, I felt something strange happening in my back, something of a "crack" occurring. I spent the night on the front room floor, trying to find relief from the pain.

Because of the continuing pain in my lower back I went to the neighborhood clinic where a temporary diagnosis of a slipped disc was made. An "erosion" of two vertebrae in the lower spine were noted, and the illium, a bone in the pelvis, looked as if it were "moth eaten."

The x-rays were sent to a specialist in Paris who suggested that nothing be done surgically. Other specialists advised a biopsy to help diagnose the malady. Through an incision in the lower abdomen, a few bone specimens would be removed from the illium and the inner side of the vertebrae for microscopic examination.

In that same October of 1969, Samuel Gerber of the European Mennonite Bible School at Bienenberg, Switzerland, was scheduled to hold meetings at our church. I wondered if the biopsy could not be delayed until the meetings were concluded. My doctor agreed.

On a Sunday afternoon of those weekend meetings, an anointing service was held at my request. Most of the members of our tiny congregation attended the simple service held in our apartment under the direction of Samuel Gerber. He explained to the congregation that there was nothing magic about anointing with oil. It was simply an act of faith following the teaching of James 5 in the New Testament. With hands placed upon me, with oil on my head, with prayer from the group, God was asked to heal me, their pastor.

The next day the biopsy was performed. In three weeks we learned that it was positive. How was I to feel about all this? Remember, my wife and I had committed my condition to the Lord. For us that was sufficient.

The anointing had been done; the meetings were over; Samuel Gerber was back in Switzerland. And I was in the Curie Hospital in Paris for more tests, x-rays, and consultation with a team of doctors, all in an attempt to decide what was best for me, the afflicted one. But strangely, the afflicted one now considered himself un-afflicted. I really felt confident that I had been healed, my faith hurdling the biopsy.

Although the diagnosis had been made, the medical staff involved in my case decided to seek more confir-mation, some additional weight of evidence. They would perform a sternal puncture (removing a small portion of marrow from the breast bone) as one more verifi-cation of the diagnosis before treatment began.

They made the sternal puncture. It was negative! There was no verification of cancer. This was in De-cember, 1969. It was our Christmas present.

An American surgeon who had trained at the Curie Hospital and was visiting there at the time was called in for consultation. He suggested that in America an

illium puncture would be made. At the French doctors'
request, he performed this. It too was negative!

Various other tests followed: immuno-electrophoresus,
x-rays after injection of—I'm not sure what. Always
negative! The doctors were puzzled and begin to question their original diagnosis. However, the x-rays and
plates from the original biopsy clearly showed a disorder.
They suggest another biopsy.

It was time to give my testimony. I told the French
and American doctors that I had been healed by God.
The American surgeon from Texas, the cancer specialist,
found my explanation "very interesting." I suggested
that since I was feeling much better, the pain was gone,
and there was no evidence of active malignancy, why
not just check up on me periodically. The doctors agreed.

And so I have been going back to the doctors, to
the clinics, to the hospitals for periodical checkups. I
have done this both in France and North America when
home on furlough. The x-rays in 1971 revealed what
might possibly be interpreted as a slight deterioration
of bone, but x-rays in April 1972 showed no further
change.

My report from the doctor of the Curie Hospital on
March 12, 1973, is translated as follows:

> The results of the isotopic tests of February 12
> are reassuring. They have confirmed the two activ-
> ity centers that you had in the lumbar region, but
> have not indicated any other localizations. I will
> be very happy to see you again in three months.

To date I have had no treatment of any kind for
plasma cell cytoma.

And what of the future? I look at things like this.
If I escape death by auto accident in 1970, it doesn't
mean that I will never be killed by an automobile during

the rest of my life. I personally believe that I was healed. For how long? I do not know. I am in His hands. And that's a pretty good place to be.

To God be the glory!

Witnesses:

Samuel Gerber
European Mennonite Bible School
Bienenberg, Switzerland

Marlin Miller
44 rue Sebastien Mercier
Paris 15me France

11 HEALED AND IN A WHEELCHAIR

● Elizabeth Hart

FROM Philadelphia to Lebanon, Pennsylvania, is ninety miles. In 1952, my husband, Jacob Hart, drove those ninety miles. But later he said, "The Lord must have driven the car. I do not remember driving a single mile of the road. My heart was too full, too broken."

Jacob was taking me home. We had lived together as husband and wife for eighteen years. And now, according to the doctors at the Graduate Hospital in Philadelphia, we would soon need to part. They told Jacob that I had only a few days to live. Today, some 20 years later, I am still living but my husband has gone on to glory. It is true that I am in a wheelchair, but I still say that God healed me. My testimony is found in Hosea 6:1,2: "Come, and let us return unto

---

Elizabeth Hart lives with her son at Manheim, Pennsylvania. Although confined to a wheelchair for twenty years, she sews both as a hobby and for income, maintains an active interest in women's activities of the church, and loves to travel.

the Lord: for he hath torn, and he will heal us. . . .
In the third day he will raise us up, and we shall live
in his sight." God raised me up from what I believe
was my death bed, sat me on a wheelchair, and I want
to praise Him all the remainder of my days.

In 1952 I became severely ill with what appeared to
be multiple sclerosis. Soon my kidneys and intestines
began to malfunction. Arrangements were made to take
me to the Graduate Hospital at Philadelphia, Pennsylvania, for tests and observation.

There after a variety of tests and studies, I was wheeled
into a medical amphitheater. It was a teaching session,
and a large number of doctors sat around the edge of
that room and listened to my case being described. I
was not acquainted with all of the medical terms they
used, but I understood that my central nervous system
was degenerating. Later my Christian family physician
stated that the disease was known scientifically as "amia
trophic lateral sclerosis."

After that session, they informed Jacob that he could
take me home. Prognosis? The specialist gently told
Jacob that I could not live. How long did I have? Not
long, not long at all. And that's why Jacob, lost in lonely
grief, drove those miles home in a despondent haze.
He stopped and turned at the right places, but his
thoughts were not on driving. They were on me.

I had often read in James 5, verses 14 and 15, "Is
any sick among you? let him call for the elders of the
church; and let them pray over him, anointing him with
oil in the name of the Lord: and the prayer of faith
shall save the sick, and the Lord shall raise him up;
and if he have committed sins, they shall be forgiven
him."

Lying on that Philadelphia hospital bed, I had made
a promise to the Lord. If He let me go home to my
family, I would "give a testimony." What sort of a

testimony was it to be? A testimony of reconciliation to the death that my doctor had predicted? A testimony of healing that James had assured me was possible? I did not know what God had in store for me. I considered myself now to be in the hands of another Physician. Earthly physicians had given up, but I knew God was still able to heal.

Bishop Simon Bucher, pastor Sidney Gingerich, deacon Norman Shue, minister Isaac Baer, and my husband, Jacob Hart, gathered around my bed for the anointing service. As prayer was made, as the oil was placed upon my head, I felt the presence of God come close to me. I had no desire to get out of bed. I confess at this time that it seemed to me to be an anointing for my death.

Two days later I realized that death was near. Again, several of my dear friends mentioned above, plus my sister, Mrs. Frank Hershey, and my two teenage daughters gathered in that same room. They joined hands and prayed fervently for my recovery. Husband Jacob held my hand. I remembered their praying, then everything faded away. The consciousness which had periodically washed over me like the waves of the sea during those last days, keeping me in touch with reality for brief periods of time, seemed to roll out like the tide which waits for no man.

Later Jacob told me what happened. They checked my pulse and could find none. My body was cold. My sister cried. My daughters cried. Death seemed imminent. Their cries seemed to bring me back. I asked my husband to help me up, then fell back into a natural sleep.

Was the anointing unto death? Had God said, "I need Elizabeth Hart. I shall release her from her bed of pain"? No, God wanted my testimony to be heard by others. It was that simple. So, He healed me. It was not medicine nor surgery—just God. I believe in both medicine and surgery, but I believe that God sometimes goes beyond what these are able to accomplish. After that my body organs worked again, and I was soon out of bed. Man is limited, God is not.

I do not walk today. I am partially paralyzed in my right leg. I live with my son and daughter-in-law. God took me from my deathbed and placed me in a wheelchair. It is enough. I am satisfied. When I first found out that a book was being written about those who have experienced healing, I wrote to those concerned and said, "If you can use this testimony, you may do so. If not, I have been blessed again in giving it." And that has always been the way I have felt about my experience. I want God to be praised.

AUTHOR'S NOTE

Twenty years have passed since this plainly dressed, prayer veiled sister was healed. She was smiling then, she is smiling now, her wheelchair a throne of praise. God said, "Elizabeth, I want you here in heaven, but not just yet. Strengthen my people by your testimony to my healing grace. Tell the strangers, shout it from your wheelchair, 'Our God is a great God. He can strike down, He can raise up. Smile from your wheelchair. Tell friends and neighbors of my power. Sing aloud of my goodness. Let the unbelievers hear and wonder. Let the righteous hear and rejoice, for I am a great God and worthy to be praised.'"

Witnesses:

Norman Shue
Route 1
Lebanon, Pennsylvania 17042

Mrs. Frank Hershey
442 Willow Road
Lancaster, Pennsylvania 17600

Dr. A. H. Heisey, M.D.
1 W. Main Street
Quentin, Pennsylvania 17083

12 HISTOPLASMOSIS AND AMPHOTERICIN B

● Carolyn Graber

IT ALL BEGAN on our 160 acre dairy farm near Plymouth, Indiana. In the second week of August, 1969, when I was six months pregnant, I began to run a fever. At first the fever would occur occasionally, but as time progressed it appeared much more frequently. Finally it remained as a constant symptom, only to fluctuate by degrees for almost a month and a half.

During this time the obstetrician was having extra tests taken to determine the cause of the fever which previously had been linked to the pregnancy.

On September 25, 1969, I went into labor and delivered a premature 2 lb. 14 oz. boy. And the fever still persisted. I was dismissed from the hospital three days

---

Carolyn Graber is a busy mother and wife who along with her housework and helping on a dairy farm finds time for her hobby, reading. She summarizes her outlook on life with the words, "I must wait on God and see what He has in store for me."

later, leaving the new baby in the care of the nurses and the incubator.

After I came home, the fever became progressively worse until it was almost constant. After being at home three days, it became so bad that I knew I had to have help. I was very sick. My husband, Toby, contacted our doctor who immediately told me to go to the Elkhart General Hospital where I was admitted in the care of a specialist of internal medicine.

By this time the doctors were suspecting tuberculosis. So I was moved from a semi-private room the first night to an isolation room. Many tests were taken, tests of the blood, of the urine, a liver biopsy, bone marrow tests, and a sputum culture. The final diagnosis was confirmed two weeks later. It was histoplasmosis.

Histoplasmosis is a rare disease for this area of the country. It is caused by a fungus whose spores are carried through the air from droppings of birds, mice, and other animals. The spores are microscopic in size, so light they are easily scattered.

The spores lodge in the lungs where they produce tiny fungus plants which are responsible for this disease, histoplasmosis. In advanced cases it may spread to other parts of the body and be fatal. In my case it had spread in my lungs, scattered to my bone marrow, liver, and spleen.

The specific drug to which histoplasmosis responds most favorably is known as amphotericin B. It is not a common disease; it is not a common drug. The specialist who cared for me had dealt with only one such case before. By contacting other authorities in this field, however, a carefully prescribed dosage was prepared for intravenous administration.

The side effects of this drug, which can be fatal in itself if not administered properly and carefully supervised, are nausea, headache, chilling of the extremities, and possible damage to the kidneys. I experienced all these reactions. Afterwards, I learned my doctor expected me to live only a few more days.

But there was no choice. Drop by drop the amphotericin B was fed into my blood system.

After two days of this intravenous medication, my temperature rose to 105 degrees. My body rejected the amphotericin B. Coughing spells almost made me choke.

I had been in isolation for two weeks. I was tired of being treated as if I were some poisonous object. Everyone who entered my room wore a gown and a mask. The door was kept shut.

I was becoming discouraged with the horrible side effects of the drug. I was tempted to tell the doctor to stop the intravenous medication. It was the low point of my sickness.

Many questions worried me. Would my premature baby, Stanley, live? Would the children's home allow us to complete the adoption of six month old Larry, whom we had taken when he was ten days old? How was our four year old Curtis adjusting to different relatives as he was shuffled from one home to another during my absence? How could my husband endure this pace of farming, milking cows, other chores, preparing something to eat, and driving two hours each day to visit me in the hospital?

But even though I felt discouraged, I knew God had not forsaken me. My healing was the object of much prayer. In Nappanee two churches joined together in prayer for my recovery. Small groups were meeting and having special prayer for me.

On Saturday, just two days before my toughest round with amphotericin B, Dean Hochstetler, a member of the Bourbon Chapel where my husband and I attended, visited me at the hospital. With him came Kreshma

Boodram from the island of Trinidad in the Caribbean Sea. This dark-skinned brother is a mighty man of prayer. There beside my bed, Kreshma Boodram prayed a prayer that I will never forget. He literally commanded God to heal me.

Monday was a hard day, but relief and release came that night. For the first time in many weeks I slept in peace. Tuesday a new intravenous injection was prepared and administered. I showed little reaction. There was no more coughing. My body accepted the drug on Tuesday that it had been so violently objecting to earlier.

My medical charts were described "as if a bomb had hit them." Lines that formerly went down, turned up. Lines that formerly had steadily risen, now plummeted drastically to normal levels. Everything was "go" for recovery.

After three more weeks in the hospital to allow my body to regain strength, I went home healed. The last x-rays taken revealed something interesting. The disease was expected to leave lesions on my lungs. It is the nature of the disease. But the x-rays revealed no lesions. It is the nature of God.

Was it the drug, amphotericin B? Was it divine healing? Cannot we who are spiritual appreciate the beautiful work of the fine Christian specialist who ministered to me? And cannot we also appreciate the healing ministry of the Great Physician? It also is beautiful.

Must we only chalk up another victory for another wonder drug? Should not the God to whom so many prayed on my behalf also receive due credit?

The three Christian nurses who did private nursing for two weeks with me accepted God's healing in my illness. The specialist reminded us that this drug was powerful and effective. And he was right. However, God also was powerful and effective.

I do not believe that it was the single prayer of any

one person that healed me. He heard them all; He
listened.

I just know that God healed me! Praise God!

Witnesses:
>   Mary Ellen Kaufman, R.N.
>   Route 1, Box 332
>   Nappanee, Indiana 46550
>
>   Lorene Stichter, R.N.
>   505 N. Clark Street
>   Nappanee, Indiana 46550
>
>   Eileen Eash
>   Route 5, Box 296
>   Goshen, Indiana 46526

13 EVERYDAY IS HALLELUJAH DAY AT OUR HOUSE!

• Sue Dalton

AT 25761 Alexander St., Bedford, Ohio, which is next
door to Cleveland, sitting quietly in a closet, is a paper
sack. It contains a shoe for my left foot. That shoe has
a built up sole of one and a quarter inches. I, Sue Dalton,
am the former wearer of the shoe with the fat sole.
The shoe weighed a "ton" and was ugly. I should know.
I wore that shoe for four years, from age 14 to 18. They
were long years. Those are such difficult years to be
handicapped. Classmates at school can be cruel, very
cruel. But I had to wear it to correct a bone growth
deficiency in my left leg.

The history of the ugly shoe can be traced back to
the beginning of my life. Certainly, I wore it not by
choice. I was a victim of cerebral palsy from birth. Brain

Sue Dalton has served one year in Voluntary Service under the
Mennonite Board of Missions. At the time of this writing she was
living at home and attending the Lee Heights Mennonite Church in
Cleveland, Ohio.

surgery at an early age left me with only my left side
slightly impaired. My general appearance, health, and
mind were fine. However, when I reached the age of
14, I began to have one dislocated knee after another.
And always it was my left knee. A visit to my orthopedic
surgeon brought sad news. My sudden growth at this
age was not proceeding equally in my two legs. The
left leg fell behind, and tests showed that I would need
to wear a corrective shoe with a thick sole on my left
foot. It was a tremendous adjustment for a 14 year old
girl to make and proved a real handicap in my teenage
activities. But eventually I adjusted to the situation,
reconciling myself to wearing that type of shoe for the
rest of my life.

On May 7, 1972, a girl friend asked me to accompany
her to hear a minister named Angely in Akron, Ohio,
at the Grace Cathedral. The minister preached on faith
and I wondered if he was speaking to me. He invited
those who wanted healing to come forward. The girl
friend who took me to that meeting was also handicapped. She was nearly deaf in one ear. We both went
forward, one not hearing aright, one not walking aright.
And there we stood, wanting so much for God to heal
us of our infirmities.

What did I think of as I stood there trembling, seeking,
hungering? Did I think that God could heal me of that
shortened leg? Listen, when God healed my girl friend
of her deafness that night, when she could really hear
out of that ear that had never responded properly to
sound before, then I knew He could heal me.

The minister had me remove the shoe with the built
up sole. I walked for him, my steps faltering, limping.
Then he prayed for me and I felt my legs go numb.
I thought I would fall, but did not. I felt God all around
me, supporting me. When the prayer was finished, I
took a step, a step of faith in more ways than one. I

tried to walk. That first step was perfectly normal, no falter, no limp. I took another step. It was like when I was a little girl. I ran. God had healed me. It was as simple as that. No light from heaven, no clap of thunder, just a simple, wonderful healing by the Great Physician.

I graduated from high school on June 7, 1972. Graduation was important to me, but I believe it was more important to my parents. Mom and Dad said their hearts overflowed as I walked across the platform like other girls to receive that diploma. Now I run, ride my bike, swim, "goof off" like other kids. God is good, so very good.

Recently I attended an orientation school in Elkhart, Indiana, for young people who were entering a period of voluntary service under the Mennonite Church. We serve in hospitals, children's homes, in relief work throughout the United States and Canada without pay. I wanted to do this. I thought it would be a way of showing God how grateful I was to Him for His healing. At that orientation school I shared with other young people what God had done for me. From there I left for New Hampshire to work in a country home for the aged. The shoe with the thick sole stayed in Cleveland, Ohio.

Others say they notice no limp when I walk. Before, when I took that shoe off and tried to get along without it, I suffered severe pains in my back. Today, there is no shoe, no pain. People ask me, "Do you really think that God healed you?" And I say with joy in my heart, "Yes, God healed me."

My mother says, "Since our daughter was healed, everyday is hallelujah day at our home!"

And why not? When the lame man was healed by God through the ministry of Peter and John that day at the gate of the temple that is called Beautiful, he "leaped up, stood, and walked, and entered with them into the temple, walking and leaping, and praising God." I have been healed by that same God, so I am doing that same thing. "It's really cool now. When I go to buy a dress, I don't have one knee below the hemline, the other above it!"

Are all things possible to the one who believes? Or was Jesus just kidding the people of His day, playing the role, acting the part, the smooth faker of the first century? To me, such thinking is blasphemy. Jesus was the Healer, is still the Healer. I know. He touched me. Praise God! To God be the glory.

Witnesses:

Leo J. Miller
21880 Louis Road
Bedford Heights, Ohio 44146

Charles Laird
Missile View Trailer Park
Titusville, Florida 32780

14 BOTH DAUGHTER AND MOTHER

● S. Jay Hostetler

GOD IS NO RESPECTER of persons or places when it comes to healing. He heals all ages. He heals in all parts of the world. I would like to testify of two healings—one of our daughter which took place in Dhamtari, India, when she was two and one-half years old, and the other of my mother which took place in Shipshewana, Indiana, when she was seventy years old.

I have not shared these experiences with anyone, and I am a bit hesitant to share them even now. They were intense, personal happenings. However, if they can be a blessing to others, then I have no right to be quiet. If people will praise God because of them, then I must speak up. When Ida, my wife, and I prayed for God's healing hand upon our dear ones, we were not hesitant

S. Jay Hostetler, a retired missionary, served 21 years in India and seven in Ghana, West Africa. He holds both a B.A. and B.D. degree, has served in several pastorates in the United States, has taught Greek at Goshen College, Goshen, Indiana.

in making our request known to Him. God heard our prayers at that time, and I believe the Holy Spirit would have me now share with others of how God richly blessed us in these two varied situations.

At this writing, I am seventy-two years old and God has called Ida home to be with Him. I know that she would want me to share how God healed our daughter and my mother. I do not know why God did not heal my wife when we prayed, but we both told the Lord we were willing to accept His will. I claimed as His child the right to plead for her. And so I prayed for her, and many others did also. But God chose to take her. The Lord gives, and the Lord takes away. Blessed be the name of the Lord.

It was 1929. My wife and I were serving on the mission field in India. It was the cold season. One chilly afternoon in November, our two and one-half year old daughter, Mary Ann, developed a cough. At that time we were staying with the P. A. Friesens, missionaries on the same field. We thought little of the cough when it first developed. After all, Mrs. Friesen was an M.D., and certainly equipped to take care of little emergencies such as this one.

The cough increased in intensity during the succeeding hours, but it was such a gradual increase that we were hardly aware what was happening.

But when P. A. Friesen came back from his leper clinic, he was alarmed at the labored breathing of the child, more alarmed even than his doctor wife. He said with fear in his voice, "It reminds me of the breathing of our daughter who died of diphtheria in this very house sixteen years ago."

But even with a doctor in the house, the situation became serious. The magic of penicillin and streptomycin were still in the future. P.A.'s concern added to ours.

An air of tenseness permeated the little missionary bungalow.

As we stood by the child, suddenly she stopped breathing. P. A. Friesen dropped to his knees and prayed for the child. She was able to catch her breath again, but it was still a touch and go affair. Our daughter refused to eat anything solid and we were able only to force a little liquid into her swollen throat.

For two days the crisis continued. Mary Ann's breathing was so labored it could be heard from the road, 150 feet away. It was impossible for the child to take medicine orally. There was no medical complex to take her to, no iron lung into which to place her, no specialist to call in. Medical facilities on the mission field at that time were very limited.

We tried to ease the breathing with crude vaporizers constructed on the spot and by applying poultices to the tiny chest. Dr. Troyer, also a missionary on the field, arrived from another station, bringing the medical instruments to perform a tracheotomy if necessary. Mary Wenger, a registered nurse, helped in the vigil. My wife, Ida, and I did not sleep. We spent the time in prayer.

On the third day the child grew steadily weaker, her finger tips turning blue for lack of oxygen. On the third day, as parents we were finally able to pray, "Lord, if You want this daughter of ours, You can have her."

As soon as we said this we both felt strongly that we should change the poultices more rapidly, keeping them hot continually. We took that common inspiration to be a message from the Lord. We checked with Dr. Friesen, who by this time was reconciled to the child's death. She agreed that it could do no harm. We began immediately the rapid changing of the poultices.

In half an hour the child began to breathe easier. The tide that was relentlessly sweeping the wee life away was reversed. The child was healed. But before the healing came a surrender by us as parents. It seemed that God was able to work His miracle of healing in our daughter only after we, like Abraham, had become willing to offer the child to Him. When man dangles at the end of his rope, and knows that it is the end, then God has the freedom to intervene.

Mary Ann is now married and lives in Oakland, California. She is the mother of two sons and one daughter. She served in Japan as a missionary from 1952–1956.

The second miracle of healing involved my mother. We were home on furlough from India in 1945. I was called to Shipshewana, Indiana, to hear the sad news that x-rays revealed a cancerous condition in her large intestine. Although it had not become necessary to hospitalize her, she was 70, under constant sedation, and not expected to live. The doctor in attendance advised that her condition would steadily worsen and that stronger drugs would be necessary to contain the pain.

My mother, Mrs. Lizzie Miller, had remarried after my father's death. The children of those two marriages, plus our spouses, gathered at her home. My stepbrother and I anointed her with oil and then we all knelt about her. There she sat on her favorite rocker, we her children and spouses surrounding her, hands clasped, forming a prayer circle. All of us prayed for her healing. Then, mother prayed. She calmly told God that she had tried to serve Him faithfully, and now she was expecting God to be faithful to her.

At the close of that prayer, a prayer some of the children thought rather presumptuous, my mother, who had been diagnosed as having terminal cancer, looked around the circle and testified that the pain was gone. The next day she arose, went briskly about her housework, and said that she felt "as light as a feather." She passed a mass of unidentified material in a bowel movement.

When mother did not return for continuing checkups, for the stronger sedatives that were indicated as the disease progressed, the doctor contacted her by phone. The physician feared that she had gone to a cancer quack for treatment. In reply to the doctor's inquiry, Mother joyfully confessed that she had been healed, that there was no further need to see a doctor for this particular ailment. The doctor, however, insisted that she return for further x-rays. The "light as a feather" woman agreed. She went in for the x-rays.

The x-rays were taken at the Elkhart General Hospital. Where the cancer had appeared formerly, only scar tissue showed. Another physician was brought in to examine the x-rays. He agreed with Mother's doctor that there was no evidence of any cancerous growth at that time. When the puzzled doctor said, "Undoubtedly the cancer will return; this is only a remission," the consulting specialist said, "I am not sure that it will return. Sometimes things happen that we do not understand."

Mother lived for thirteen more years, dying at the age of 83, not from cancer, but from a stroke. Her testimony was that she felt better those last thirteen years of her life than she had for many years before.

Do not tell me that there is no such thing as divine healing. To me, divine healing is real. God restored to us our daughter on the mission field of India and my mother in the quiet little town of Shipshewana, Indiana. From the gates of death our daughter returned, and God by surgical means unknown to man operated upon mother and removed her cancer. Jesus said that some have ears to hear, but they do not hear; they have eyes to see, but they do not see. I have both heard and seen. Praise God!

Witnesses:

> S. Jay Hostetler
> Greencroft Villa
> Goshen, Indiana 46526

> Percy Miller
> Shipshewana, Indiana 46565

> Florence Friesen, M.D.
> Schowalter Villa
> Hesston, Kansas 67062

15 THE NURSE WHO WAS HEALED

• Rhoda S. Lapp

As A registered nurse, I am, of course, convinced that
healing takes place through the use of medicine. I am,
also, equally convinced that there is a healing from a
different source, of a different nature, a healing that
comes only through God's almighty power. This is the
healing that was demonstrated so clearly by the miracles
of Christ when He was here upon this earth, a healing
now being manifested as a result of a new outpouring
of the gifts of the Holy Spirit in these recent and perhaps
end times.

My experience with divine healing was not as dramatic
as some. My illness was not terminal. And perhaps you
would feel it is scarcely worth sharing. But I feel dif-
ferently. My God is One who intervenes in the smaller

Rhoda S. Lapp, a registered nurse, lives at Lancaster, Pennsylvania.
She attended Eastern Mennonite College, Harrisonburg, Virginia, and
received her R.N. from Riverside Hospital School of Nursing in
Newport News, Virginia. She enjoys writing as a hobby.

things of life also. He is a God of little people, ordinary people.

And I want God to get the glory for what He did in my life. Psalms 29:2 says, "Give unto the Lord the glory due unto His name." We are ready to praise the miracle drugs of today. As a nurse I know of them. But as a Christian nurse I also know of God's healing touch. So I can praise the goodness of God as well as the power of penicillin.

Although it has been three years since God healed me, the events of that night and the days that followed are sparkling clear to me.

On Friday evening, February 19, 1971, my husband, John, and I went to revival meetings which were in progress at the Bethany Mennonite Church near Goodville, Pennsylvania. Fred Augsburger from Youngstown, Ohio, was the speaker for these meetings.

The minister at Bethany, Herman Myers, had charge of the devotional period that night, after which Brother Augsburger spoke briefly. Then he led us in a song. He paused for a moment and said, "The Spirit of the Lord is telling me that someone in this audience has problems here." He laid his hand across his chest. "I don't know whether it's heart trouble or not," he continued.

John and I were sitting in the back. I looked over the audience. No one budged. Since we were strangers there, I didn't know if anyone else had a chest problem or not. But I knew I did.

For a number of years I had had asthma attacks which practically incapacitated me. Frequently I used an inhalator for relief. In addition I took medication, but I tried to avoid the medicine when possible because of the bad side effects it had upon me.

As I looked at Fred Aubsburger that night in front of the Bethany Mennonite Church, hand across his chest,

I thought of something else. I thought of the pain I had been having in my chest for some time, a pain that seemed unrelated to the asthma.

As a nurse I have watched many patients die of cancer. I have seen them suffer through surgery, often repeated surgery, followed by radiation treatments. I have observed the toxic effects of chemotherapy. I have watched them waste away. And I will admit I feared cancer more than any disease I have encountered on the hospital wards.

I knew I must face up to that pain in my chest, a pain that seemed to be growing. Yet in spite of my medical training I put it off. That night in church Fred Augsburger helped me to see myself more clearly, to recognize the error of procrastination.

"Would you come up front? The Lord wants to heal you," Augsburger invited.

John tapped me on the shoulder and whispered, "That's you!"

My heart pounded loudly. Could he possibly mean me? No one else went forward. But how would it look, myself a nurse, to walk forward and seek healing from a man whose profession was preaching, not practicing medicine?

Slowly, after a moment's hesitation, I rose from my seat and walked down the aisle. I wondered what this preacher would do to me, what the Lord would ask me to do next.

Augsburger asked me to kneel in front of the altar. Then he asked if anyone in the audience who would like to come forward and lay hands on me while he prayed.

I heard footsteps coming down the aisle in back of me. There was no mistake. I recognized the footsteps of my dear husband. The minister at Bethany also came forward. The two of them stood beside me. The evangelist stepped down from behind the pulpit. Then there were four of us.

Next I heard Brother Augsburger ask the people in the audience to join hands and pray. While my husband and the two ordained men placed their hands on me. And then I heard the evangelist pray for my healing. I sensed the intense concern of the entire audience. The prayer committed me to God. I felt blessed.

I went back to my seat.

After the service was over, Brother Augsburger shook hands with me in the rear of the church. He asked me if I could sense any difference.

"I can't tell for sure," I said, "since most of my problem is at night and on Saturday when I try to do my housecleaning. I can tell you tomorrow.

"Should I throw away all my medicine and really believe God?" I asked him.

"No," he replied. "Sometimes God heals instantaneously and sometimes gradually. Wait on the Lord. See your doctor."

As a nurse I was happy to hear him say that. I thought I heard him saying by such a statement, "We need practitioners of medical science. We must not despise them at all. But God sometimes can offer us something that goes beyond the skill of specialists."

I went to bed that night with my inhalator beside my pillow as usual. But I didn't need it.

The next day, Saturday, I ran the sweeper and did my weekly house cleaning without relying on my inhaler as I usually did. And sometimes that even was not enough and I had to take an asthma pill too. (One of my allergies was house dust.) But this Saturday I didn't need either. Frankly, I was amazed.

We were having company Saturday evening for supper and also for Sunday dinner. I worked hard to prepare for them. By 5:00 p.m. Saturday I was extremely weary and completely exhausted, but not wheezing or feeling short of breath as usually was the case when I over-exerted myself. I must confess that I was still surprised, but oh, so grateful!

The phone rang and I answered it. Brother Fred Miller, the Sunday school superintendent from the Landisville Mennonite Church where John and I attended, asked me if I would give my testimony at church the next morning or give a few comments on the Sunday school lesson. I was amazed again. This man didn't know a thing about what had happened and he was asking me to give my testimony.

It was as if God was asking me to share my experience. The Sunday school lesson for that day, February 21, 1971, was "Knowing and Doing God's Will." I accepted his assignment and decided to share what God was doing in my life.

That morning in church I testified that I had experienced God's leading as I became a Christian, as I became a nurse, as I became the wife of John Lapp.

But I admitted that I had always been reluctant to burden God with requests for physical healing. I was never willing to commit my illnesses to Him, to seek His healing, to ask for His touch, for Him to supplement the medicines I took. I consulted God about many things, but not about my illness.

Then I proceeded to tell the congregation at Landisville about my unusual experience at Bethany on Friday evening and my freedom from wheezing in spite of an exhausting schedule the previous day.

I said that I felt so unworthy of what God had done for me and that I didn't deserve it. I also mentioned that I didn't know why God heals some people instantaneously, some gradually, and some people by taking them home to heaven.

I believe God's timing was in that telephone call that

came to me less than 24 hours after I sought God's healing. I believe that God wants us to share with others our faith in Him. And so He provided the opportunity.

It has now been several years since I accepted God's healing in my life. Satan does not want me to write of these things. But I am sharing them here so that God may receive glory for what He has done for me.

As a nurse, as one trained in the healing arts, as one who has accepted Christ's call to minister to others, I have always tried to be intellectually honest. That I was allergic to dust, various pollens, odors of oil, gasoline, and certain perfumes is beyond question. They triggered severe asthmatic attacks.

The pain in my chest, the pain that I feared might be caused by a malignancy, of that I am not certain. Recent x-rays of my chest reveal no evidence of any anatomical anomalies. I feel that God healed me of whatever caused that pain. And I am so glad He did. No longer do I fear cancer either. God took the fear away too. Praise God! He is physician, surgeon, psychiatrist. He is everything to me!

I acknowledge that Satan has power. But I believe the power of God, the blood of Christ, exceeds the power of Satan. I believe that Satan would have me doubt, but I believe that God would have me trust. I have come to believe that there is physical healing as well as spiritual healing for us in the atoning blood of Christ.

As I look back on the night I sat in the Bethany Mennonite Church, I realize that I really needed Brother Augsburger to call me out of that audience for healing in my lungs. My faith would not have been strong enough to ask for healing and receive it. And, at that time I was wrestling with the thought, "It may not be God's will to heal me." Since Evangelist Augsburger had received the message from the Lord, that was my guarantee that the Lord wanted to heal me, that He would heal me.

You might ask, "But how do you know that this evangelist received his message from the Lord? Perhaps it was his own thought."

My feelings along this line are simple. I believe that God works today, just as He did in biblical times, through men and women who are yielded to Him, who are filled with His Spirit. So I trust such people in the brotherhood.

Could it be that the Lord would like to bestow this gift of discernment and healing on some more of us for His glory and the edification of the church?

Would we be glad to accept it, or would we be afraid of what people might say or think of us?

Witnesses:
> Herman Myers
> Route 1
> East Earl, Pennsylvania 17519
>
> Mrs. Kenneth Shearer
> 453 Mt. Sidney Road
> Lancaster, Pennsylvania 17601

16 HEALED WITHOUT ASKING

• Ruth Martin

DURING the summer of 1969 I contracted a severe eye infection. My husband, Aaron, was in graduate school, and we were on a shoestring budget. I neglected going to a doctor for about a week. When I did the doctor diagnosed the condition as iritis, and did not hold out any encouragement at all. Even with cortisone injections, he indicated that he could not promise that much vision would be restored.

And yet the Lord was kind. With heavy dark glasses I could get around in a week or so, and continued to improve for a couple of months. After a year the only remaining effect was extreme sensitivity to glare which I was told would be permanent. In the daytime I had to wear very dark glasses to avoid severe headaches and loss of vision. And driving at night for me was

---

Ruth Martin has a college degree in Spanish and Greek, a husband astronomer who teaches in a junior college, four children, and she lives for the Lord in Upland, California.

totally out of the question as the bright lights against the darkness would black out everything. This, I was told, was the result of dead tissue being white and scattering the light rather than absorbing it. I would have to learn to live with it. With four children, one less than a year old, there were some problems, but no really serious handicap.

It never occurred to my husband and me to ask the Lord to change things. We felt that His hand had prevented total blindness and made it possible for me to care for my family. I thought perhaps the glare-blindness was left to remind me of what He had prevented. And I was grateful for what God had done.

In the summer of 1971, two years after that original eye infection, my husband finished his Master's program in San Diego, and we needed to find a job. We had hoped the additional study would prepare us for a church assignment. We contacted every mission board and service outlet with negative results. There was no place for us.

We sent out applications to more than 100 schools and colleges all over the country and received only one response. We moved from our beloved San Diego to the Los Angeles area in search of a job—any job. We had never moved previously without a clear sense of the Lord's leading.

Several months after our move, desperately discouraged about having no close fellowship and no chance to serve the church, we were on our way to visit friends in San Diego. And God spoke to us in a miraculous way on the Los Angeles freeway during rush hour. What a strange place for the Lord to minister to us!

It was dark. Four packed lanes of traffic were being funneled into one to get around an accident. The headlights blinded me. The pain and tension aggravated my sense of loneliness and depression. As we crept along the freeway, I prayed in desperation, "Lord, we're only trying to follow You. If we're not *completely* on the wrong track, couldn't You give us *some* kind of encouragement? I can't go on like this!"

I don't know what happened then or why, suddenly, as if a switch had been flipped, I could see clearly— headlights and all. The pain was gone. I could see road signs and watch the cars' lights, a beautiful chain of diamonds and rubies where moments before I perceived only a blinding glare.

I told Aaron about it. Neither of us quite believed the change was for real. That weekend we were with the best friends we have ever had, and told no one. I guess we weren't sure that it would last. If faith were the condition for healing, we would have flunked for sure. We had not even asked for healing, and God gave it to me.

But it did last. Two years later my sight is even better than it was before the infection.

The Lord has taught us many things through this experience. We still have not found the service assignment we've longed for these dozen years. We are still seeking the fellowship of another family that is eager to pursue intense and far reaching ways of following the Lord and sharing together.

But we have seen His power and His love in new ways. Everytime I take the car out at night I am reminded that God has a reason for our being at this spot at this particular time. He made it unmistakeably clear that we're *not* headed in the wrong direction. When all was dark, He sent light. May the Lord receive praise.

Witnesses:

Mr. and Mrs. Guy West
3857 Westgate Place
San Diego, California 92105

Mr. and Mrs. C. T. Daub
6160 Mohler
San Diego, California 92120

17 LUMPS IN THE ABDOMEN

● John Otto

I LISTENED with surprise as the doctor in Oklahoma City said, "Your blood tests came back. They were satisfactory. But you have several lump-like masses in your abdomen that should not be there. I would like to admit you to the hospital for x-rays, further tests, and possible surgery. I'll check to see if they have a room available at the hospital this afternoon."

Lumps in the abdomen? Enter the hospital this afternoon? Just a minute! I was joining my family that afternoon for a weekend camping excursion. They were already at Muskogee, Oklahoma, some ninety miles away. The State Prep Baseball Championship Tournament was being held there and my oldest son was playing in it. I had to join them there that afternoon. I explained the situation to the doctor.

John Otto, a pastor and father of five children, enjoys golfing, reading, woodworking, sports, camping, and traveling. His motto: "Each day is a gift from God. Use that gift to please the Giver."

"Well, all right," he agreed reluctantly. "But be sure that you check into the hospital on Monday."

The ninety mile drive to Muskogee gave me ample reflection time. I had gone to the family doctor for a routine annual medical checkup. Now I was faced with the prospect of being hospitalized again. But the question that really kept tumbling around in my mind was the reason for the hospitalization: lump-like masses in the abdomen. Cancer?

It seemed that our family had already put in their quota of time in the hospital. For me it had been stitches in the head, a cast on the leg, an appendectomy, an ugly burn on the leg, all requiring hospitalization. And then I was admitted with a severe stomach ulcer. When I left the hospital that time, I left three-fourths of my stomach behind.

Edna, my wife, had a difficult delivery with our first child and major surgery at the birth of our second child. Our one son had broken both a leg and a hip. I thought, "Lord, it's hardly my turn to go in again!"

I was the son of an ordained Amish minister. I sowed my wild oats like many of the young men of our faith. I did so until I was arrested by Jesus Christ at Sarasota, Florida. Through my girl friend, the Lord led me to the Mennonite Church.

Since the age of ten I had sensed God's call to become a preacher. Encouraged by Tim Brenneman, pastor in Sarasota, prodded further by Edna and the Lord, I put the house up for sale. I laid out the fleece.

And God replied by a letter from Cherry Box, Missouri, with a call to pastor a small church. So the ex-Amish boy with an eighth grade education found himself standing behind a pulpit.

Later, God opened the way for me to further my education for several years at Hesston College, Hesston, Kansas. Then I was called to an emerging church in

Spencer, Oklahoma. In addition to pastoring the church, I operated a lumber and hardware business. The strain was too great. After repeated but unsuccessful attempts to sell the business, I resigned the pastorate.

But God was still dealing with me about that early childhood call. I talked with Howard Zehr at Mission '72, a North American mission conference that was held at Hesston, Kansas. I shared my feelings with him. He encouraged me to complete a questionnaire and application form indicating my availability as a pastor.

I had mailed that letter to Howard Zehr the morning before I went to the doctor. As I drove that afternoon to Muskogee, Oklahoma, to be with the rest of the family, the past came rolling back. And I thought, "So now, Lord, there are lumps in my abdomen. Why, Lord?" Perhaps I shouldn't have mailed that letter.

I tried to convince myself that nothing serious would result from the upcoming hospital visit. My middle age pot belly belied the possibility of cancer. I was gaining weight, not losing it. True, I tired easier in recent days but that was because I was working so hard.

At Muskogee, Edna was not so optimistic. I sensed her deep concern. The ball game was played, but no longer did it seem so important.

The premonition lurking in the back of our minds that those lumps in the abdomen were cancer were soon proven right.

X-rays on Monday and Tuesday led to surgery on Friday. The doctor told Edna on Tuesday that she should brace herself for the inevitable. He did not expect me to live for more than several weeks. He told her that the growths had increased significantly in size in the few days since that first examination.

Edna brought the two oldest boys up to the room to visit me. I could see their bewildered and tender looks, but I didn't know how much they knew.

On Friday I was in surgery only a short time. The cancer was widespread. The surgeons could not remove the growths. A little of the tissue was removed and sent to the lab for analysis.

Many visitors and flowers came to my room after word was out that my disease was terminal. Many prayers were offered, many cards sent, many comforting words spoken.

Two visits meant more to me than others. One visitor told me that death by cancer is kinder than death by accident, since a slower death would give me time to get things in order. It was true.

The other especially meaningful visit came from my brother in the form of a book, *Power in Praise*. It emphasized giving thanks to God for everything. It reminded me that God was preparing me for more life—either more life on earth, or life in heaven. God removed the last bit of apprehension that I had brought along to the hospital.

The lab report came back that the cancer would respond to radiation treatment. Fresh in my mind was how radiation had shrunken a 64-year-old brother in our congregation from 150 pounds down to 99 pounds. But I resigned myself to the radiation treatments.

My family doctor sent the x-ray film, lab report, and surgical report with me to the Oklahoma University Hospital where I was to see the head of the radiology department. There I talked with five or six doctors. The last doctor to talk to me was a Dr. Shaw and I ended up being his patient at the Oklahoma Medical Research Foundation. I don't know how it was determined that Dr. Shaw would take my case. Maybe the doctors drew straws, and he happened to get the short one.

I went home for lunch then checked into the Research Hospital for a thorough examination. A team of three doctors would be responsible for my treatment. They explained that the drugs they would be using were highly toxic and would cause some bad side effects. Among other things, I could expect to develop sores in my mouth, stinging hands and feet, loss of hair, nausea, and loss of strength. They said there was a 50% chance of successful response to the treatment.

What did I have to lose? I signed the waiver forms.

The drugs were worse than I expected and after the second treatment I begged the doctors to stop them. Everything happened to me that the doctors had forewarned me of. I became as bald as an eagle. Really more so, since the bald eagle only appears bald. I was. I became much weaker.

Visitors continued to come, friends continued to pray. One day a friend brought a visitor along who had experienced a miracle healing through prayer. He had been a patient of this same Medical Research Foundation. The doctors told him that his cancer was not being checked. So he turned to God and began seeking salvation and healing. The salvation and healing came, so he equated them in his mind and decided that going back to a doctor would be a denial of his faith. So he quit the doctors. I didn't feel like that.

Another visitor came to my bedside who had had a miracle healing from cancer. He asked me to pray after him the exact words he said. And I did. But after the prayer, I told him that my spirit couldn't agree with his spirit when he prayed, "Oh God, we demand healing for this body."

This visitor told me that my sickness was an attack of Satan and that healing would come if I renounced Satan. I knew what I believed, yet as a result of such visits I began to struggle with those beliefs. My wife said that she could not control my thinking, but that I was going to continue with the doctor no matter what. Good wife.

The third chemotherapy treatment was given to me

as an out patient. I continued to feel worse after each treatment.

Then one day Bill Barnett came to my bedside. Bill was a bulldozer operator who had done work for me. As he sat there by my cot, tears streaming down his face, he asked me if I would mind if he prayed for me. I told him I would be delighted.

Bill knelt by my cot and prayed a prayer for my healing. It was during his prayer that I felt the touch of God in my body. The touch was like a light electric current moving from top to bottom of my body. Bill ended his prayer by saying, "Not our will, but Thine be done."

Before Bill left, I sat up and had a cup of tea with him. That day I knew that God was preparing me for more life here on earth.

I continued my chemotherapy treatments. I had agreed to submit myself to the program the doctors had outlined. I felt no word of discouragement from the Lord in this regard. But I knew that I was healed.

Three months and five treatments later the medical team put me through the same extensive examination that they had performed initially. How thrilling their report!

Dr. Shaw began his announcement like this: "I know you are a religious man, and I have faith in God too. What has happened here has been a miracle. We cannot find a trace of a tumor. The cancer is in complete remission."

With candor he continued, "Your case is the most dramatic case that we have in our care. We would, of course, like to take all the credit. But we know that would be less than honest when we compare you with other statistics."

Dr. Shaw told me that perhaps I was cured, but that they never talk in those terms to cancer patients until five years after the treatment, and even then they speak a 99% chance of no recurrence. Immediately following what appears to be a cancer cure, doctors suggest that there is a 50% chance of recurrence. With each passing year that the tumor is in remission the chances improve by 10%.

That was a year ago, and I have been living a normal life and working the past six months. In July we moved to Fort Dodge, Iowa, where I was called to serve as pastor. I know in whom I have believed. I know that He is able to keep me healed. I know that He wants me to serve Him some more in this world of sin.

I am taking maintenance treatments here in Fort Dodge. According to protocol I should take them for another six months. The doctors in Oklahoma City said that I might not need to continue the drugs, but their program calls for it, and they want me to continue, for added insurance. I am submitting cheerfully, willingly to their requests. I have never denied that God has used the skill of physicians and surgeons in healing my body. But I know that I was healed of the Lord the day Bill Barnett prayed for me. The doctors seek insurance; I have assurance.

In retrospect, I know that God came to me in a very special way, which causes my eyes to fill with tears. I feel like the songwriter who expressed it like this: "Who am I, that a King should bleed and die for? Who am I, that He should pray, not My will, but Thine be done."

And I guess the article in *The Way* which I read when I was in Voluntary Service sixteen years ago speaks also to the way I feel. I had just broken my leg. The article was entitled, "Why God Breaks Legs." It told how the shepherd sometimes broke the leg of a frisky lamb so that he could give the lamb the tender love and care that would always keep the reckless one close beside him after the leg had healed.

Tender love and care came to me in several dramatic ways during my illness.

One Sunday morning I was at home feeling especially bad. Edna was at my bedside as she often was. And I expressed to her that I could understand being sick, that I didn't feel I should have any immunity from sickness, but the thing that was difficult for me to accept at this time was the financial problems that were piling up.

When we sold our lumber business in Oklahoma, we took a real financial loss. I was just beginning to see the light at the end of the tunnel as far as finances were concerned, when the lumps came. How do you feed five children and pay your debts lying in bed?

Edna tried to reassure me. We would just have to trust God to work things out for us.

"Yes," I replied, "but God doesn't pay the bills, and He doesn't make the loans."

Twenty minutes later one of the brethren from our congregation brought the children home and presented me with a love offering of $714.00 from our church.

I turned over in bed and wept. I asked God to forgive me for doubting Him. I knew that offering represented considerable sacrifice, since it came from a small congregation made up of six families.

The generous help of our church and other congregations where we have been members, churches in the community, friends, relatives, Mennonite Mutual Aid with its regular schedule of help plus grants from their catastrophe funds—through all these the Lord has helped us in our serious financial crisis.

The prayers of Bill Barnett and many other Christians were honored and helped me through a serious physical crisis.

The touch of God's love truly came through His

people and I am still thanking Him for His power and presence. My desire is to express my gratitude through faithful service to Him.

All honor to Him!

Witnesses:

    Don Cox
    4500 Shadynook Way
    Spencer, Oklahoma 73084

    Moses Mast
    8417 N.E. 34
    Spencer, Oklahoma 73084

18 I LIVE IN A WORLD OF LIGHT

● Harold Buzzard

TWICE I stood in healing lines, once in Flint, Michigan, once in Mishawaka, Indiana. And men of God prayed for my healing. Once four of us, myself, my pastor, and our wives met in Elkhart, Indiana, for a special prayer service that centered on my blindness. And we asked God for healing. Once in 1973 in Goshen, Indiana, a young lady came up to our table in a restaurant and asked if she could pray for my recovery of sight. And I agreed. I have never refused the prayers of God's people.

I have been blind for over 30 years. And many, many people beyond those mentioned above have prayed for me, prayed that I might see. My wife, Alpha, has probably been the most faithful in this respect. I remember

Harold Buzzard, successful businessman and long time member of the Belmont Mennonite Church, resides in Elkhart, Indiana. Active in church work, he is an accomplished chess player, and maintains a keen interest in music.

how confident she was that God would heal me that time in Mishawaka. She sat near the front of the tent where the healing service was conducted with our only son in her arms. I had never seen that one year old child, and Alpha wanted him to be one of the first objects to light my eyes.

But my eyes were not opened. I am still blind. Today my son is 29 years old, but I have never seen him. I believe I have heard God say, "Expect no miracle." And strange as this may seem to the reader, this is all right with me. I have accepted my blindness, and that is a form of healing also. I have never blamed God, never threatened God, never begged God, never felt like giving up because God chose not to heal me. God knows best.

I was a senior in college when I first became conscious that the sight in my right eye was nearly gone. That was in 1934 and I was 24 years old. I had been near-sighted, and wore glasses to correct that defect. But to learn suddenly that half of my vision was nearly gone was disturbing to say the least. Changing lenses in my glasses helped temporarily, but soon it became impossible to correct the problem through this procedure.

In 1937, I traveled to Fisher, Illinois, where a skilled eye surgeon, Dr. George Troyer, successfully removed a cataract from my right eye. He was unsuccessful, however, in correcting for the loss of that natural lens through the use of glasses. There was obviously more to my problem than simply the opacity of a lens.

In 1941, now married, my wife and I went to Chicago, Illinois, to see an eye specialist who diagnosed my condition as retinitis pigmentosa. The retina of the right eye had deteriorated. He predicted that the same thing would happen to my left eye. The retina, that delicate lining on the inside of the eyeball, is sensitive to light and of course, necessary for seeing.

And he was right. The last year in which I drove

a car was 1941. It seemed as if a curtain was gradually being drawn across my left eye. Today I have only a slight perception of light in that eye. Some would say that my world of darkness is nearly complete.

But, of course, they are wrong—absolutely, positively wrong. I live in a world of light. My philosophy of life is found in John 8:12: "Jesus spoke to them again: 'I am the Light of the world. Whosoever follows me will have the light of life and will never walk in darkness.' " That is from today's English Version, *Good News for Modern Man.* And it is good news for me. I follow Him; I do not walk in darkness.

I would not infer that to walk in this "world of lightness" when I am physically blind has always been easy. I have passed through some deep waters. I have learned to accept some things that to others might seem minor, but to me were major obstacles.

To accept the blind person's identification mark, the tapping cane, was difficult for myself and my wife. In the early 1940's, I was a door-to-door salesman. As my blindness accelerated, I found that climbing porch steps was becoming too difficult for me to handle. One day I forced myself to take a cane along. Now I would not be without it. It is a part of me, and I do not think of it as a mark of my handicap. I accept it as a tool that enables me to live rather normally, sightless in a world of light.

Today my wife and I manage a successful janitorial supply service. We have close to 200 customers, including industrial plants, business firms, and institutions in the Elkhart, Goshen, Bristol, and New Paris areas of northern Indiana. The mobile home industry accounts for a good share of the business. I have found that a handicap does not have to incapacitate a person. God did not call me a vegetable, but a disciple.

To be blind today is not nearly so unfortunate as

to be blind fifty years ago. Through records, tapes, and Braille printing, I have access to good music and learning literature and can carry on correspondence with friends.

People ask me, "Do you think God could heal you right now of your blindness?" There is not a thread of doubt, not a shadow of question in my mind about His ability to do so. Then why didn't he heal me? I prayed, others prayed, but God said, "No." Why?

I give God more credit than certain of my critics. Some persons argue with God, question God, berate God. I cannot do that. My God, who has not healed me, is still my God of love. He loves me, and I love Him.

I believe that God saw something ahead for me, back there in the days when I was going blind. He saw the 1940's. He saw the 1950's, the 1960's, the 1970's. God saw the whole picture. He saw how Alpha could help me. He saw how I could be of help to others because of my blindness. He saw how I could be an influence, how I could give my testimony for Him in a better, more unique, more forceful way as a blind person than one with sight. Through my blindness I believe I have helped others.

So during these three decades of blindness, I have really seen. I have seen the love of my wife, Alpha, who never gave me up as a useless burden. I have seen the love of the church, of friends, of business contacts, a multitude of people.

But especially I have seen the love of God. There is no scientific way of comparing my relationship now to God as a blind person to what it would have been if I could have seen these many years. But I am satisfied that my blindness has drawn me closer to Him. My blindness has helped me to see God more clearly, to sense His tender love and compassion.

In my blindness I praise God for light!

19 HEALED AT COMMUNION

● Margarito Bustos

I HAVE BEEN a diabetic for many years, the first symptoms arising in 1966. It is an illness that apparently runs in our family, since many of the Bustos have problems that center in those pancreatic tissues where insulin is secreted.

My most recent trouble started in November of 1972. It began with a little pain in the bottom of my feet. In a week's time the pain seemed to have spread to all parts of my body.

I called my doctor and he said it was probably the London flu. He prescribed medicine, but after taking the medicine for a week, the pains were worse.

Twice I was taken to the hospital. I received pills and shots that seemed to help some. The pains in my

---

Margarito Bustos, better known as "Mac," pastors the Spanish Mennonite Church in Moline, Illinois. He is the father of two children, follows football and baseball, and sees life as "an opportunity to serve other people."

123

upper body left me, but never those in my legs from the knees down. They stayed until the Lord healed me.

The doctor decided that I had had a stroke, and that it had affected my nerves, especially those in my lower legs. He sent me home with plenty of vitamins and some of the strongest pills for pain that he was allowed to furnish me. I took them every six hours.

Days, weeks, and months passed. I was getting worse—the pains were unbearable. I could not sleep, except for a few moments at a time. Nights were a nightmare. Although I was tired, I couldn't sleep long until the pain awoke me. Walking, sitting, lying down—no position gave me relief from those pains.

The last three months of my illness I couldn't drive; I couldn't preach; I couldn't do anything. Having served in the Marine Corps, I decided to go to the Veteran's Hospital at Iowa City to see if they could do something for me.

After a few days there and careful examination by three doctors, I discovered that they couldn't do anything for me either. They gave me the same vitamins and pain pills that I had been taking.

One doctor did say, "The human body is like a machine. In your case, you are using too much power with this machine to raise your legs. Soon you will need to have braces on your legs."

I was sent home with plenty of vitamins, plenty of pain pills. I was miserable and discouraged. I couldn't even read my Bible because of the pain. I felt like crying.

Yet God was giving me grace. During that week of April when I was healed, He was able to take much of my self pity away. I began to forget about myself. I prayed for other people who were sick. I started to collect my thoughts, especially about my pastorate. The sheep of my church needed a shepherd who could walk.

who could lead them. I made up my mind to send a letter of resignation from the ministry. I even decided when to send it. I would send it on April 16, 1973.

Those were my plans. I knew I could not function as a pastor the way I was. But God had other plans for me.

It was beautiful the way God led me to my healing experience. Actually, it was at a women's meeting held in our church the weekend before the Monday on which I planned to send my letter of resignation from the pastorate at Moline, Illinois.

Some sixty women from the Spanish churches in our denomination had gathered at Moline for fellowship, sharing, and counsel in Spanish. It was the first time in our church's history for such a meeting. I knew that in the afternoon session the Lord's Supper would be celebrated with the symbols of bread and wine. Deep in my heart I felt a desire to go and take communion. I thought this would be the last time I could take communion with a group of people in our church.

My brother, Mario, helped me get to the church. My wife was surprised to see me and said, "What are you doing here?" It was a good question. I don't think that any of us at the time knew the full answer—except God.

Two men and my wife helped carry me up the stairs and seated me at the rear of the church in a cushioned chair. I sat there thinking about my wife's question. Why was I there? I only wanted to take communion. I knew lots of people in that group had prayed for my healing, but I did not come with that in mind.

Many people have asked God for a miracle. And they expect a miracle. But in my case, I wasn't expecting a miracle. I never dreamed that this was the day God had set apart for my healing.

I waited in pain for the communion service. I waited

for three hours. I was taking my pain pills every thirty minutes, but had no relief from the pain. I tried to get my mind off my pain.

A lady from Indiana had dreamed about me several nights earlier. She had called my wife, Mary, just a few days before this meeting, asking how I was. She said a voice, God's voice, had been telling her to pray for me, that she felt I should be anointed with oil for my healing.

I wondered if this sister in Christ, and others who were praying for me, fully understood my problems, my physical ailments?

I knew my wife understood. She seemed to suffer as much as I, perhaps not in body, but in soul. She knew my sorrow of heart, my pain of body, my inner turmoil because God had called me to the ministry, and now I felt that I could no longer serve Him in that call.

Finally four o'clock came. Maria Snyder came to me and said, "Mac, we ladies would like to pray for you after communion." I went to the platform, helping myself along by grasping the benches as I struggled forward.

My brother, Mario, also a pastor from New Paris, Indiana, was in charge of the communion service. He had accompanied his wife and other ladies to this meeting. He distributed the emblems, the bread representing the broken body of Christ, and the juice, His shed blood.

And as I drank that communion wine, I thought of how Christ's blood was spilled for us, how by His stripes we are healed.

A strange feeling came over me. After I drank that wine, I felt something leave my body.

The ladies gathered around me, many of them placing their hands on me as I knelt, while the rest made a circle about them, holding hands, and all praying for my healing.

And then the miracle happened! I stood up and said, "I have no pain!"

They said I jumped into the air twice. I don't remember that, but I do remember going up and down the platform, praising God for His healing. At that moment it seemed like the whole atmosphere was filled with the presence of the Lord and everyone started to praise God in a loud voice. What a wonderful experience! I could scarcely believe it myself. The pain which had been with me constantly for three months was gone. I was free of pain.

People don't understand the size of that miracle. I had been taking pain-killing medicine at 12 times the regular dosage with little help. From my knees to my feet I had felt constant pain; now it was gone! I left my pain pills at the altar that day.

Even my diabetes improved. I went from 50 units of insulin a day to 16 units. The doctors were amazed. When asked if I had experienced divine healing, one doctor said, "Possibly." Another said, "Something supernatural happened."

Some may say that it was only a psychological boost that I received on April 14, 1973. As I write this six months later, I'm still free from pain. And it left me when prayer was made for me. I know that not all divine healing is instantaneous. For me it was.

I believe in miracles. Praise God!

Witnesses:

Mrs. Lester Yoder
2361 45th Street
Rock Island, Illinois 61201

Mrs. Donna McKelvey
1335 W. 13th
Davenport, Iowa 52800

20 THE DOUBLE CURE

● John W. Shank

I REMEMBER clearly the first warning I had of my hearing impairment. On a Sunday afternoon, my wife, Irene, and I were standing at the front door of our home, saying goodbye to guests. And I heard what I took to be thunder rolling across the Virginia countryside. I said to my wife, "There's a summer storm acoming. Listen to that thunder."

Wife Irene looked at me in surprise and said, "Why, John, there's no thunder."

Yet I had heard it. After seventy years of living one ought to be able to recognize thunder. But there was no thunder.

From that day in 1969 until my healing in 1971 I

John W. Shank lives in the beautiful Shenandoah Valley of Virginia. He is 74 years old, and a long time member of the Weavers' Mennonite Church. He enjoys gardening, lawn care, and home maintenance in addition to half-time maintenance job at Eastern Mennonite College.

was to be plagued by strange, rough, intermittent sounds that seemed to originate both inside and outside my head. It was frightening, incapacitating, a come and go affair that gave me no warning. The only relief I could find was to lie flat on my back. It played havoc with my nerves. After all, when you hear things and others do not, you appear strange to them. You even appear strange to yourself.

I consulted our family physician. He referred me to a specialist in Harrisonburg, Virginia. The doctor examined me and said, "There is no solution to your problem. The eustachian tube which leads from your throat to your middle ear is no longer functioning. It is non-correctable."

And I went home deeply troubled. I feared that the strange noises I heard would pry and tear at my emotional well being.

I went to another specialist in Charlottesville, Virginia. I felt that I must have relief. After an intensive examination, his diagnosis was the same. There was nothing he could do for me. No modern drugs could solve my problem. No surgery would help. No cure was known. I prayed for strength to bear that which I thought I could not bear.

And, as if that was not enough, God handed me another cross to shoulder. After a growing shortness of breath and pain in my chest, I went back to our family physician for examination of this additional problem.

His diagnosis of the new disturbance was confirmed by another specialist. In addition to my hearing problem, I was suffering from emphysema. And like before, the doctors offered no hope of a cure for this condition.

Emphysema is a lung ailment, often associated with heavy smoking. As a boy I had tried unsuccessfully to smoke one cigarette. It was my first and only attempt at smoking. Then why did God allow this disease to afflict me? Wasn't my hearing problem enough of a load to carry?

My wife and I prayed about this. We were both in our early seventies and realized physical faculties slow up as one grows older. And we accepted that. We did not pray that God would stop the normal aging process, but rather that He would give relief from these two pressing weights under which I was beginning to stagger.

God gave no sign that He heard our prayers. We trusted, but there was no healing.

Our Lord works in a variety of ways among His children. Sometimes He ministers His healing power like a bolt out of the blue; sometimes it comes gradually; sometimes there is no physical healing. But always there is spiritual healing and renewal for those who truly seek His will in their lives.

I know too that sometimes God heals through individuals, sometimes through groups. We err when we tell God how and when He must work in our lives.

I must confess that I often asked during those tension-filled months, "Lord, why am I afflicted like Job of old?" And finally the answer came, "It is for My glory."

That answer did not take away the pain, but it gave me something to which to cling. Perhaps God would be glorified if others saw me accepting these burdens with Christian grace. Or, perhaps God would be glorified in a special healing of my infirmities through the prayers of the church.

I expressed to my pastor, Alvin Kanagy, an interest in having special prayer by the Weaver Mennonite Church on my behalf. I said, "Let the brotherhood pray for me."

I made that request with care. It is easier to ask God in the privacy of one's home for healing. Then there is little explaining to do if the prayer is not answered.

But I believe that sometimes God calls us to make our wishes known publicly, to stick our neck out for the Lord.

And so we did. We decided to ask God for a special healing, to lay out the fleece, to seek a definite answer.

On Sunday morning, July 25, 1971, a group from our church met to have special prayer for my healing, for my double healing. They came to the fellowship hall beside the church, the building called Shady Oaks. They came before church; they came fasting; they came praying.

That morning, right after the regular worship service, I was invited to the front of the sanctuary. And there a number of brethren gathered around me, placed their hands upon me, asking God to heal me twice, to heal my hearing, to heal my breathing.

I had told the pastor, "Let no one pray for me except those who believe that God can heal me." And so it was.

But nothing happened. The noises were still there. The lungs still toiled to take in their oxygen.

And yet I felt that God had healed me. I thanked Him for it. I knew that God would either heal me or give me a better plan.

That day in the Weaver Church I felt that I was the most unworthy person there. And yet I sensed that God cared for me, that the brotherhood cared. If God would have done no more, that would have been enough. It was like at my conversion. I knew that I had met and experienced God's love afresh. I left that church with the assurance of God's healing power in my life.

And four months later God validated my trust in Him. On November 1, 1971, the noises disappeared. Why on November 1, 1971? I don't know. I just praise God that the daily noise, the resulting nervous tension, left me. I experienced the healing for which I had trusted God.

God honored my faith. He glorified Himself. My healing did not come when I expected it. It came in God's own good time. The specialists had said, "There is nothing we can do." God said, "Wait on me, and I will bring it to pass."

I waited four more months, expectantly waited for the second miracle. And in March it came.

Spring was arriving in the Shenandoah Valley. A new season was beginning. And with it came new life for me. How strange the way God works. How wonderful His acts. How unexplainable.

Again, I can remember the exact day. It was March 1, 1972. I had rejoiced in God's previous healing, but I did wonder why He only healed my hearing. Why not my emphysema? I knew He was able.

I had grown used to shallow breathing, even breathing with pain. It had become a way of life with me. But on that day there was no pain. I breathed deeper. There was still no pain. I could hardly believe it. It was wonderful. I sampled lungful after lungful of air. There was no trace of pain.

I said in amazement to my wife, "Irene, I'm missing my emphysema. I can breathe clear down to my belt and there's no pain."

I went to Harrisonburg for re-examination and x-rays. The specialist said, "I find no trace of emphysema." Praise God!

For healing one needs faith. I feel that I am blessed with it. My son asked me, "Dad, how do you get a faith like that?"

I told him how I felt that it came from reading the Scriptures, pleading for faith, knowing that He could give it. And so God gave it to me.

At this writing I am seventy-four years old. I work at Eastern Mennonite College, Harrisonburg, Virginia, doing maintenance. I am active, trusting and praising

God daily, thanking Him for each painless breath, for each true sound that I hear. I have not asked God for a lifetime of healing, to slow the aging process. But I had the boldness of faith to ask Him for a double healing of my body. And, just as He heard Elisha's request for a double portion of Elijah's spirit, so He heard me.

Some say that my problems left by natural means. To me that would be a strange way of looking at things. Good physicians said they saw no solution to my problems. We prayed, and I was healed. It seems like a simple cause-effect relationship. I am a simple man, so I can accept a simple answer.

God heard me, the least of all His children. How good He is!

Witnesses:

Alvin Kanagy
Route 5
Harrisonburg, Virginia 22801

Glendon L. Blosser
Route 5, Box 181
Harrisonburg, Virginia 22801

21 FROM CONFINEMENT TO FREEDOM

● Alva Swartzendruber

ON FEBRUARY 15, 1970, I took my car to the body shop for repairs. And from then until April 15, I remember nothing. God blocked two months from my life. During that time I was in a hospital and convalescent home, but I recall nothing of it. People talked to me and I answered, but I cannot remember the events or the conversations.

My son tells me that a Lutheran minister came to my hospital room after he saw my name on the register as a new admission. He prayed with me. After his prayer, I prayed. My son was there and remarked after my recovery, "Dad, I never in my life heard a more beautiful prayer from you." And I recall nothing of that visit.

During that February day when I was attempting to get our car repaired, I suffered what the doctor later called a "slow stroke." I don't know. To me it seemed

---

Alva Swartzendruber was born in 1899 and is one of the older minister-bishops of the Mennonite Church, living in Kalona, Iowa.

like a pretty rapid affair. It was as if I was anesthetized and placed into a time capsule for those two months.

There was five inches of snow on the ground the day I left home to take the car to the garage. The grass was green the day I looked out the window of the convalescent home, conscious for the first time of my surroundings after two months of total disorientation.

The day of my stroke, the family took me to the hospital. They could see that I was not myself. After eleven days, I was placed in a convalescent home, considered helpless and hopeless.

They tell me I gave them lots of trouble at the Pleasantview Home. I was uncooperative. In fact, I became so difficult to handle that they placed a strait jacket on me and tied me in bed. But I still managed three times to get loose. That's no way for a preacher and bishop to act, but I was not myself. To me my instantaneous recovery was a miracle. It was as if God punched a button in my brain, connected some loose wires, and reality once more flooded my soul.

On April 15, 1970, after those many days and nights of blackness, I saw a light. It got brighter and brighter. I said to myself, "Is this the glory of the Lord?" And in one sense it was. God was demonstrating His power, bringing glory to Himself, as He shook me out of my long slumber.

My eyes began to orient themselves to my surroundings. At that moment I looked out the window. I expected to see those five inches of snow on the ground. My mind began functioning where it left off that day in February when I took the car to the repair shop.

But there was no snow on the ground. It was April. Now I was confused. "Lord," I wondered, "what's happened? Where have I been? Where am I?" I lay there perplexed, trying to put things together. It was like a puzzle with some of the parts missing.

In about a half an hour the nurses came in and I inquired what day it was. She paused, startled, then told me it was Wednesday. She was shocked to have me do or say anything sensible.

I explained that I wanted to know the day of the month.

"It's April 15," she told me.

And I knew that I had been "away" for two months.

The nurse left and came back to say to me, "Alva, we have done everything we know to do for you, but we have to have cooperation from you."

When I asked her what she was talking about, she patiently explained about my climbing over the railing of the bed, getting loose from the confining ties they placed upon me, crawling out of bed, and repeatedly falling flat on my face.

I said to her, speaking carefully, earnestly, "Nurse, if I remain myself as I am now, I'll do everything you want me to do, and I'll not do anything you don't want me to do."

It was too much for the nurse. After all their trials with me, I guess she didn't think it made sense for me to talk sense. She called my doctor in the next town.

He came, examined me, saying cautiously, "Alva, you are doing all right."

I wondered why he didn't say more. Some time later I learned he had discussed my recovery with others, and expressed the belief that it was only temporary. After all, I was 76 years old at the time, well past my three score and ten.

In two weeks the doctor was back. I was still myself. He again examined me and then backed up a bit in his evaluation. He said, "Alva, I have never in my life seen a man recover like you did."

I thought it was a good time to tell him something, so I said, "Doctor, I had too many people praying for me." When God heals, I believe in telling others about it.

At that time I had still not been allowed to walk. When placed in a wheelchair, I was still tied in place. People had a hard time accepting the fact that the once obstreperous patient was now a lamb. It was difficult for some to believe that God was healing both body and mind.

But after the doctor left that second time, I asked to go to the bathroom across the hall. The nurse wanted to help me, but I said, "I can walk by myself." She questioned it, but let me try.

And after those months of just lying and sitting, only falling when I escaped from my bed, I walked across the hall as good as I have ever walked. Of course, that's my opinion, but a bishop's word should be good!

I am up every day; I am enjoying every day. Although I am still at the Pleasantview Nursing Home, I do not think of it as confinement. I may live here, but I am not the same.

I occasionally go into Wellman where I work at repairing hydraulic jacks. When God brought me back from my state of suspended animation, He did not intend that I just sit around twiddling my thumbs.

I still preach whenever I am asked, filling appointments for absent ministers. God is not finished with me yet, so I keep plugging along.

I think God is wonderful.

Witnesses:

    Ruth Eash, R.N.
    Pleasantview Home
    Kalona, Iowa 52247

    Dr. Jay R. Miller, M.D.
    310 8th Avenue
    Wellman, Iowa 52456

    Carl Smeltzer
    Kalona, Iowa 52247

22 PERHAPS A YEAR

● Nelson Kanagy

I HAVE LEARNED to live one day at a time. Time is precious to all of us, perhaps more so to me. Some would say that I am living on borrowed time. I prefer to call it "God-given time." My life is in His hands.

Twice I have placed my life in the hands of surgeons. I thank God for all those who have dedicated their lives to the healing arts. I'm glad they take their work as seriously as I take my calling to preach the Gospel. I have faith in such men.

But I also have a great deal of faith in God. And sometimes He overrules from heaven the wisest predictions of medical specialists. It has now been over eighteen years since I received the grim, but honest words, "From a short-range view, expect a normal recovery

---

Nelson Kanagy, long time pastor and church worker, lives in Sarasota, Florida, where he has "temporarily retired." He says that his activities are "visiting the sick, caring for my invalid wife, and doing what I can for others."

from this operation. The long-range view is not so optimistic."

"How long?" I asked.

"Perhaps a year," he replied.

Sad news? Actually it was better than what I had received from my previous surgeon.

It was in 1954 when I was pastor of the Oak Grove Mennonite Church in West Liberty, Ohio that I first noticed the symptoms that led me twice to submit to the surgeon's knife, ending with the evaluation, "Perhaps a year, not much more." I suppose they thought that was plenty of time for a pastor to get his house in order.

I had some pain in my abdomen in 1954, an area that seemed more rigid than the surrounding tissue. I went to a physician, who examined and questioned me. Knowing my background, the pressure upon me, he recommended a vacation from the pulpit to give my body time to relax and rest. Most pastors are under a nervous strain. I was no exception, and the doctor's advice was in order.

We took a five week vacation and I honestly tried to free myself from the burdens of pastoral responsibility. But the "pressure" remained.

A high fever developed after our vacation and I returned to the doctor for further examination. It was now possible through palpitation of the abdomen to identify a lump of tissue that seemed foreign to the body. Surgery was necessary to check if it was malignant. And I submitted to that surgery in early July, 1954.

The surgeon's prognosis was not pleasant to hear, regardless of whether one is a minister or not. He had removed as much of the malignancy as he dared. Understanding the implications of the cancerous material remaining within me, he estimated my remaining life to be a matter of weeks rather than months—certainly not years.

My surgeon did recommend a colleague at the University Hospital in Columbus, Ohio, who might be willing to consider further surgery. I entered the University Hospital in August, 1954, and after one week submitted to surgery for the second time.

I want to pay tribute to the Oak Grove Mennonite Church where I was pastor at the time of my hospitalization ordeals. When the church first heard about that initial surgery in July, 1954, when the gloomy forecast was given for my future, most members were in the middle of the busy farming season. They left their machinery in the fields and gathered at the church to pray for me. Every pastor needs a praying church and I thank God that was my kind of church.

After six weeks at the University Hospital, I returned home with only a slightly better report than before I went. The surgeon who operated this time gently suggested a year more of life. And that was prefaced with a "perhaps."

I returned to the surgeon after eighteen months and he expressed his surprise at seeing me. I had outlived his estimate by six months. "I honestly did not think you would live," he admitted. "But you must remember that a whole church was praying for me," I told him. He said quietly, "That may be the answer."

For me, I know it was the answer. The skill of the two surgeons could only accomplish so much. I am writing this in 1973. I feel that God extended my years like Hezekiah of old. In that case, the Almighty God Himself told the king he would not live, then reversed Himself, and gave Hezekiah fifteen years more of life. My own death was predicted for about 1955. But God chose otherwise. For me, it seems as if God matched Hezekiah's fifteen years and threw in three more. Every year is a gift from Him.

The surgeon's predictions were based on their experience and training. They went as far as they could, admitted their humanity, and told me honestly what to expect. I appreciate their honesty, their skilled hands that ministered to me. I feel that God still had work mapped out for me to do. I continued my ministry at the Oak Grove Mennonite Church for a number of years. Then God called me to the Bay Shore congregation in Sarasota, Florida, where I served for five years. Since 1971 I am resting. If God wants to use me again, He will let me know.

As I look back on my healing experience, my heart is full. I learned much from that experience. In 1954 when things looked dark for me, June Hostetler, a sister in that Ohio congregation, gave this simple, yet bold prophecy: "He will be healed." And I was healed.

A minister expects to serve, to bear the burdens of his parish. At Oak Grove I saw the other side of the coin. I found myself accepting the ministry of my church members, the ministry of prayer. They interceded with God for me, pled my case with Him, and God listened.

I am living today on the time that God gave me because a church gathered to pray for me.

Witnesses:
>
> Martha Miller, R.N.
> Mary Rutan Hospital
> Bellefontaine, Ohio 43311
>
> Mrs. Fred Kauffman
> Route 2
> West Liberty, Ohio 43357

23 MY DELAYED HEALING

● Harvey R. Zimmerman

IF YOU had talked to me before 1970, you would have needed to be on the right side of me. Otherwise, I could not have heard you. That is, unless you would have spoken loudly, or I could have read your lips. I suffered from a 90% hearing loss in my left ear. That's just 10% away from deafness.

Can you imagine what that is like? It means that many of the beautiful sounds around you will not be heard, at least not in their fullness. Your world is more silent, but also more dull. It means that when you talk to people, you must position yourself; in public meetings you must always sit in the left side of the auditorium.

A hearing loss of 90% in one ear is like having only one ear. Listen to a record, to a radio, to a speaker

---

Harvey R. Zimmerman, a building contractor by trade, lives in East Earl, Pennsylvania and attends the Bowmansville Mennonite Church. He is married, the father of four children, and enjoys golfing as well as big game hunting.

with a hand over one ear. Notice the difference. It was like that for me, only I didn't have to place my hand there. For me to hear only 10% of something through that ear was normal every day of my life. Every day, that is, until the blessed day in February, 1970, when God healed me of my near deafness in that ear.

My problem had been with me since I was a boy of 12. I had a ringing in that ear and drainage from a damaged ear drum that would not heal for seventeen years. Like the woman with issue of blood in the Bible, I had seen many doctors. A mastoid operation in 1969 brought no significant change in my condition, no improvement in my hearing.

Fred Augsburger, a Mennonite evangelist, was in our area of Pennsylvania for a series of meetings. My wife attended the services faithfully. I did not. She asked me to go. She told me about the response of the people to the evangelist's call for spiritual and physical healing. Finally, I said, "I'll go." Then not too seriously I added, "Maybe the Lord wants to heal me."

That night at the close of the service, Fred Augsburger called for people to respond to the gospel, to the healing Man from Galilee. And he said, "The Lord reveals to me that there is someone here with a hearing problem."

Wow! I waited for my wife to punch me, to whisper, "That's you." She didn't. I was on my own. No one needed to remind me that the evangelist was talking to me. I didn't want to go forward. But I did.

At the front of that church, Augsburger asked me about my problem. When I told him about the deafness in my left ear, he said simply, "Hallelujah! The Lord told me also that it was your left ear."

He placed one hand on top of my head, the other on my deaf ear, and there in the front of the Bethany Mennonite Church prayed for my healing. It was a simple, straightforward prayer, made in faith. And I knew that God was there, that He loved me, that He cared about my pain of the past, my handicap of the present.

Yes, I felt God's love. I believed that He would heal me, that He had healed me. Yet nothing happened. I still could not hear from that ear. And still I believed. But why couldn't I hear if I had been healed? Where was the proof, the evidence of my healing? Was the healing service just an emotional affair? I couldn't believe it was simply that.

I had gone to that meeting, a doubter, nearly deaf in one ear. I came away a believer, yet still without my hearing. Is that what they call a paradox? I have only an eighth grade education. I am largely self-educated. Perhaps it is easier for people like myself to believe in God, to place their faith in Him, if they are not burdened by many years of schooling. Jesus seemed to have better results in His ministry to publicans and harlots than He did with Pharisees and Saduccees. I don't know. I do know that I believed.

Two days later I testified of my healing, and yet I could not hear one bit better out of that ear. It was a strange thing to say, a strange way to feel. I believed that something had happened, but people to whom I talked wanted more than a belief. They wanted proof. And the only proof that I had was the way I felt inside. And that is pretty difficult to share with others.

That evening after having given my testimony, I felt some distress in my ear. I did something that sometimes gave me some relief. I gently forced air from my throat up my Eustachian tube to my middle ear, holding my nose shut all the while.

I felt a "pop" in my left ear. And I could hear out of it! The proof of my healing was delayed 48 hours, but now it was there, so real, so beautiful.

Two weeks later, when I saw my doctor, he remarked

about how smooth my ear drum was compared to the previous time that he had examined it. I asked if he would give me a hearing check. He did. My 90% hearing loss had improved to 25%. He was surprised. I wasn't. I felt that I should tell him about my healing experience. But I didn't. Sometimes it's difficult to talk with doctors.

It took me six months to get up the courage to tell my doctor about having been "treated" by a person without medical training. I remember so well his reaction. He leaned forward, placed his chin upon his hand, and said several times in amazement, "This is interesting. This is very interesting." When questioned later whether my case could be classified as an example of divine healing, he said, "It is questionable." But I do not question it.

To me the experience is more than interesting. It is beyond questioning. It is a miracle. My hearing loss is now only 10% in that ear. What a dramatic improvement over my 90% hearing disability. I can't argue with that.

Some people would tell me that in process of popping my ear, the pressure disturbance corrected some physiological impairment of long standing. I have read much about the ear—the tiny delicate bones of the middle ear, the curled snail-like cochlea of the inner ear, the marvelous auditory nerve that carries nerve impulses to my cerebrum, where the vibrations that enter my ear canal are interpreted as sound with all the inflections, tones, variations, and pitches involved. I have difficulty understanding how my simple exercise could correct a difficulty of 17 years.

But even if that were the case, God's timing was a miracle. Personally, I simply believe that God healed me. I can understand that with an eighth grade education.

Witnesses:
Melvin H. Lauver
1033 Broad Street
Akron, Pennsylvania 17501

Mahlon Zimmerman
Route 2
Ephrata, Pennsylvania 17522

24 LET GOD'S HEALING POWER BE RELEASED

• Clare F. Schumm

THREE OF US rode in the car that Friday, March 23, 1973. From Indianapolis, Indiana, to our home in Elkhart in the northern part of the state is 130 miles. It was a time of great emotional stress for Katie Ann and myself. The distance seemed endless. Our hearts cried out for our daughter, Darla, the third occupant of the car. As parents of that innocent seven year old child, we did not feel that we could accept the burden the specialist at the Medical Center had placed upon us. As Darla's parents our spirits united in protest to God.

We longed to get off to ourselves and release the tears that were dammed up, threatening to burst forth in raging, scalding torrents. But we did not want to break down in front of our daughter. Already she had asked

Clare Schumm is a native of Ontario, doing double duty in the United States. He serves as pastor-leader of a three-man ministerial team at the Sunnyside Mennonite Church in Dunlap, Indiana, while enrolled at the Mennonite Biblical Seminary in Elkhart.

why Mommy had cried in the doctor's office. And we had explained the best we felt we could how Mother was sorry about Darla's eyes, that she could not see as well as other boys and girls.

Back in Elkhart, Katie Ann and I did get off by ourselves. And we cried. It was hard for both of us. As a father, as a minister, perhaps outwardly I bore up a bit more bravely, but inside I was emotionally in turmoil. It hardly seemed fair for God to ask this of us.

The two hour testing of Darla's eyes at the Indiana University Medical Center seemed like the end of a long, cold journey. And when we arrived, instead of a warm fire to kindle the hope within us, we found only cold, gray ashes.

For some time we had noticed that Darla held her books quite closely for reading, that she practically sat on the television set when viewing it. We asked the school nurse to check her eyes. The nurse referred us to an optometrist. The optometrist suggested an eye specialist. The specialist sent us to the I.U. Medical Clinic at Indianapolis. And there the search seemed to come to an end. And there we found ashes instead of warmth, despair instead of hope.

After a two hour examination, after consulting with his colleagues, the doctor informed us that it appeared Darla had Stargardt's Disease. Basically this is the result of a defective optic nerve that failed to develop. It involved both eyes. Peripheral vision in this disease is satisfactory, but sharpness of frontal vision is considerably impaired.

Our daughter's vision tested out at 20/200 instead of the normal 20/20. Treatment would not help. Glasses wouldn't either. That's when Katie Ann broke down and cried in the doctor's office. And I would have liked to do so also.

The doctor at the University Medical Clinic in Indianapolis suggested that we come back the following Wednesday for "Grand Rounds." This would be an opportunity for many doctors, specialists, residents, and interns to examine Darla further and confirm or disprove his diagnosis.

I am a pastor at the Sunnyside Mennonite Church in Dunlap, Indiana. Some years ago that church was destroyed by a tornado that howled through this area. And now a tornado was scouring our souls.

I am also enrolled in the Mennonite Biblical Seminary in Elkhart, Indiana. As a pastor, as a student, I was to be the shepherd figure in the congregation. But now in the darkness of this hour, I needed someone to lead me.

We shared with a few people in the congregation that Sunday the heaviness of our hearts. And on Monday I entered the office of J. C. Wenger of our seminary. He is an esteemed brother in the Mennonite Church, a man of great faith and wisdom, possessing the gift of discernment, of giving and receiving counsel.

I asked this professor-brother how we should pray in this matter. Should we pray for complete healing, demand it of God, insist that He prevent this catastrophe, that He halt it, that He remedy it? Was it God's will that our child be so afflicted? Should we ask for an anointing service? How do you pray for something that you cannot accept?

Bishop Wenger suggested we pray that God's healing power might be released and that we try not to let our concern upset Darla. A seven year old doesn't have many years of experience and maturity upon which to draw. We prayed in his office, and J. C. Wenger later shared our need with the seminary community.

Tuesday we will not quickly forget. That day at the seminary, our regular chapel speaker did not appear.

John Howard Yoder, president of the seminary, suggested that the chapel time be used as a period of prayer for our daughter. It was a moving experience to feel the concern from approximately fifty of God's servants, professors and students, as they tarried before the Almighty One for Darla.

In addition, we knew of many from the Sunnyside congregation, our relatives, and other friends who also were interceding for us. We needed those prayers, every one of them.

There was at the Seminary a man of God from Indonesia, a country where the Lord has been much at work. He came to our home in this hour of need.

He shared briefly with us, seeking to affirm our faith, our willingness to search our own lives for hidden sin, our desire simply to ask and accept from God what was best for our child. And so our faith was affirmed, our lives searched and our desire expressed.

He prayed for us in English. And later he prayed for us in an unknown tongue. He prayed for the enlargement of our faith. He prayed for Darla.

And the agonizing burden under which we labored for the past days, from Friday to Tuesday, lifted. Praise God! It is impossible to tell you the depths of the agony, despair, and frustration which had gripped our lives. We had not been able to accept the burden laid upon us. It had been too much.

And neither can we tell you through words on this printed page what happened that day the brother laid his hands upon us and prayed. Katie Ann described it as the removal of a heavy weight which she had carried on her chest that long weekend. And we knew that we felt at peace with God. It would be possible from that moment to live with whatever God allowed to come into our lives.

Later, with our permission, with Darla's okay, our

Indonesian brother returned and prayed specifically for our daughter.

On Wednesday we were back in Indianapolis for "Grand Rounds" at the Medical Center. Twenty-six doctors observed and examined Darla in rapid succession.

There was a half hour long conference. And then a strange report. The doctor said, "We are baffled. We cannot find sufficient evidence to identify the difficulty as Stargardt's Disease. We suggest further testing, including an electroretinogram." By their questioning we could see that they were considering the possibility of other difficulties.

We went back to Elkhart this time rejoicing. We felt that our daughter was being healed.

But the ways of God are not fathomable by man. We cannot plumb the depths of His understanding. We cannot plot His will for our lives, nor measure the distance He would have us journey. We cannot see the mountain peaks ahead which He would have us climb. But we sense the shadowed valleys.

And so the summer marched along. There were momentary testings of our faith, shakings, quiverings, but each time God restored us to the plain of trust where He wanted us to be. And it was where we wanted to be also.

Because of a breakdown of vital testing equipment at Indianapolis, further examinations of Darla were postponed. We were anxious for additional medical evidence of her healing. Or, if there was to be a new diagnosis, we wanted to know of that. To believe in God, to look to God, to trust that God cares for us, does not mean that we forswear medical skills and help. We were still concerned about our daughter's vision. If she did not have Stargardt's Disease, what was her problem?

About this time, we learned of medical facilities available to us at Ann Arbor, Michigan, operated by the University of Michigan Medical School. We understood that a physician of top repute in diseases of the eye, a Dr. Falls, practiced there.

We consulted with our local specialist about seeing this man. He hastily told us that, although this was possible, it would take many months of waiting because of the heavy demands for his service.

He made contact for us, however, and in a short time we had an appointment. God is always on time.

At Ann Arbor, after a thorough examination, Dr. Falls confirmed that Darla had Stargardt's Disease. But he had words of assurance for us. He told us that our daughter would never go blind, that she would always be able to take care of herself, that she could progress educationally as far as she chose.

The disease is a hereditary one, caused by a recessive gene carried by both Katie Ann and myself. Our children would have a one in four chance to have this disease, two out of four chances to be only carriers like ourselves, or a one out of four chance to be completely free of the disease.

Our daughter, to the best of our observations, has accepted her present condition. And as her parents, we have also. We know that continuing adjustments will need to be made. For Katie Ann and me, God appears to be sufficient.

People ask us, "Now, where do you stand on this matter of divine healing? You were so happy when you came back from Indianapolis that second time early in 1973. Then you had no definite diagnosis. Now the disease of which you thought your daughter was being healed has been confirmed. So where are you at?"

And I tell them of Luke 11:1-13. The disciples asked Jesus, "Lord, teach us to pray." And he did.

And Jesus has been doing that in our lives. We don't

know exactly what He has done in the life of Darla. But we know that He is working in her body and mind even as He works in ours.

We believe in asking, in seeking, in knocking. We will not limit God. We will continue to ask Him for His perfect will to be accomplished in Darla.

Of one healing we are positive. To us it was divine. God healed Katie Ann and me emotionally, mentally, spiritually, psychologically. We have walked through the valley of the shadow of death, and we fear no evil.

As a pastor, this experience has enabled me to relate better to my congregation. When the heart of a wife aches as she discovers her husband has terminal cancer, my heart aches with her. I understand the unspeakable pain within such a soul when she sobs, "How shall I pray?"

I can comprehend that anguish far better today than in the past. And I am able by God's grace to help others to pray.

As Christians, Katie Ann and I believe there is healing waiting for all of us. And to some in the brotherhood God has given the special gift of timing, of discernment, of reaching out with a healing touch that connects us with God.

As young parents we covet the prayers of all of God's people. We seek only His will in our lives and in the life of Darla.

He will work things out to His glory and to our good. For the two to occur together is not an impossibility. Praise God!

SECTION THREE

THE EPILOGUE

DIVINE HEALING: REALITY OR FANTASY

I began this study with little knowledge of the field I was entering. I had a simple premise, a belief that God heals. I tried to be open. I chose not to read widely in the published works on divine healing.

It has been an interesting trip, gleaning, asking, begging, seeking, attempting to evaluate where the action is, out in the field, away from the ivory tower.

I have traveled in darkness; I have been illuminated from above. I have trudged the footpaths; I have danced on the King's highway. I am amazed at God's grace; I am ashamed of my own ignorance. I have been exalted; I have been brought low. I have experienced again man's total inability to understand and explain away the paradoxes one discovers as he makes his spiritual pilgrimage.

And in it all, I have found God sufficient. My puzzle-

ment about God's will does not diminish God. It mag-
nifies Him.

I still believe in divine healing. And I have learned
a few things.

The spectrum of attitudes on this subject among believers is characterized by its diversification. It is banded,
slotted, ranging from the shallow to the deep, from the
narrow to the broad, from the microscopic to the infinite.

The Shallow Faith

That the belief of some is limited to a peculiar circum-
stance. Divine healing becomes the court of last resort,
just beyond acupuncture. When all else has failed, when
the specialist has sadly reported that he can do no more,
then the person with the incurable ailment is turned
over to God. There is nothing to lose.

To me, this seems like a shallow faith, one that ripples
only after the cold winds of medical honesty have swept
the soul's surface for the last time and a deathlike calm
prevails. Then in desperation the shallow faith people
turn to God. Perhaps, just perhaps, God will provide
a cure where the surgeon's knife has disappointingly
failed. It's worth a chance, so they gamble on God.

Surely there is nothing wrong with the Christian seeking aid from those trained in the medical skills. But
neither is there anything wrong with that Christian seeking counsel, guidance, healing from God at the same
time. God is present in the hospital as well as in the
church. God works through men and women in white
as well as men of the cloth. God even used the heathen
nations to accomplish His purposes in the Old Testament. Certainly He can work through the doctor or
surgeon today regardless of his faith. In divine healing,
it seems to me that God is more concerned about the
faith of the one who is ill and the one who is praying.

The person of shallow faith seems to hold God in

the background. Prayer comes after penicillin, not at the same time or even before. First the physician, then the pastor; first faith in the doctor, then faith in the divine. There is no attempt to blend the prayer of faith with the skills of Hippocrates and Galen. God becomes the god of the extreme unction, of the final rites, the last opportunity.

The Narrow Faith

I have chosen to use the word "narrow" to describe the faith of some as they apply it to divine healing. It is an extreme which to me likewise seems precarious, scarcely tenable. My fear of it may reveal my own limitations of faith. I refer to people who refuse to "darken the door" of a doctor's office.

Their faith in God is so intense and demanding that it isolates them from dependency on any other source of aid. To them God jealously demands a faith that is unspotted from aspirin or hypodermic needles.

Like the people of shallow faith, they have learned to compartmentalize God from medical and dental science. In fact, they are even more careful and sharp in their division. Between God and the doctor they place an impassable gulf. They begin with God and end with God, never shifting to place confidence in man's ability to restore the ill to health. In their eyes faith is a narrow, pure connection that goes from man to God with no possible side excursions to men or women in white.

Such people insist that God intended for Christians to seek healing only through the laying on of hands, the anointing with oil, the ministry of those who have been given the gift of healing through the fullness of the Holy Spirit. Here are the people who turn their orthodontia problems over to God, and also trust Him to fill their dental cavities. They are willing to discard their prescription eye glasses. They refuse to take their insulin. They are the people whose ready answer for the person not healed by the prayer of faith is the simple, all inclusive, and condemning, "You did not have faith."

This group seems to be saying, "God alone heals. Pin your faith on Him. If you stay ill, it is because of the sin of unbelief." Although accused of "having faith in faith," they would insist that their faith is in God.

I would like to be clear regarding this classification. I do not see in this group only the uneducated. Nor is it typified by a rural, pentecostal church of the south where poisonous snakes are handled and doses of strychnine swallowed as a test of Mark 16:18. Their beliefs are strongly anchored in verses such as Mark 11:24, Matthew 21:22, Mark 9:23, James 5:15, Phillippians 4:13, and John 14:12.

The faith of these people seems to exceed what would be termed, "the reasonable," "the normal," perhaps even that which would make "common sense." And although I cannot subscribe to their deliberate avoidance of seeking medical help, yet I am willing to acknowledge that there are facets of their faith that shine forth as the morning stars.

I am also conscious that their restricted faith, or "stubborn" faith, seems at time analagous to a man refusing to admit that two plus two equals four. The Christian faith is not a call to forget that God expects us to do some thinking on our own. I do not believe that becoming a Christian outlaws common sense.

From the person of narrow faith we hear rather frequently that healing pivots on the hinge of faith, the faith of the person who is ill. If physiological impairment still exists after prayer has been made, then the problem centers with the person who did not take up his bed and walk. He is obviously guilty of the sin of unbelief. So the person who still suffers physically is asked to accept another burden. Since God cannot be blamed, and the one who is praying is also innocent, evidently the guilt rests on the sick one. He does not believe in that which he so desperately wants. It is a cruel circle.

I personally find this approach impossible to accept. I have included in this book illustrations of people who have accepted their incapacities with Christian grace and even joy. And for them this is a healing that perhaps in some ways far exceeds the return of lost sight or use of some body part long in limbo.

To place a crown of thorns upon the person not healed seems at the least to be judgmental, perhaps macabre, yes, even malicious. He who recklessly places such a crown upon every man who does not "see" or "hear," may be in deeper need of healing than the one he so callously condemns.

The Abiding Faith

So I would speak briefly to yet one other class of people in the divine healing spectrum—those of abiding faith.

How I rejoice in those whose faith in God is so abiding, so deep, so everlasting that their bed of pain becomes a dais for rejoicing. Healed or not healed, God is their strength and victory. They live rejoicing; they die rejoicing. God is their refuge, their sustenance, their fortress. He is their shepherd, a light in the dark valley of suffering.

Such people in affliction are stronger than we who walk about in good health. They shame us with their constant, abiding faith. We go to their home or hospital to comfort them, and we are the ones who are comforted.

Every reader of this book knows of such people. They are afflicted with cancer; they are not healed. They are resigned to God's will. And when death comes, when God calls them home, they go with a song of praise on their lips.

They never demanded of God, they never insisted, never threatened. They simply accepted. And in the simplicity of "not my will, but Thine be done," they became Christ-like.

Do I advocate a shallow faith, a narrow faith, or an abiding faith? It is a rhetorical question. The answer is obvious.

Clarifying My View

I presume that some readers will now classify me as a "middle streamer" in the river of divine healing. I paddle the center. I do not cling to one bank and insist that there is no other side. There is danger when clinging to the bank of being swept into a tiny bay where the water stands and stagnates.

I believe that the simple adage, "God helps those who help themselves," applies at this point. May I illustrate with an earthy example? You can perhaps think of a dozen of your own.

My brother-in-law and his family from Long Island, New York, were visiting us in the Midwest. While they renewed friendships with others in the community, my brother-in-law asked me to mind his dog which they had brought with them. He left it in my personal care. The dog escaped.

Since my brother-in-law is blind, and the dog was his constant companion, it was a tragic situation. We were desperate. We searched for it, but could not find it. In the days that we looked for the dog, we tried a variety of advertising media, we scoured the neighborhood. We alerted our friends in the area.

And we prayed. Earnestly prayed. But all the while we kept searching and trying to think of the best method of retrieving a frightened dog for a heartsick man.

God rewarded both our prayers and search. The dog was recovered. There was a joyful reunion of Flicka and my brother-in-law. And we all bowed our heads and praised God aloud that He cared for us and for a dog. Both the search and the prayer were important.

Similarly God calls me to back up the physician's skill with prayer. I am neither ashamed of consulting God, nor of consulting my doctor. Nor have I heard any member of the medical profession say too loudly, "Rubbish," for such an amalgamation of talent. No doctor has ever said to me, "I will treat you only if you disconnect yourself from your God." And neither has God demanded that I disassociate myself from the physician and his drugs before He will listen to me. God has never made it an either-or situation.

A dependency upon God and upon medicine does not seem to me to be an impossible union. I subscribed to God as a youth long before a physician prescribed for me as an adult. And I believe that God honors both the subscription and the prescription.

Honest in My Disappointments

Although I do not believe that God is limited in His ability to heal, yet I am bothered that reported divine healing cases seem most frequent in disabilities related to the circulatory system, limbs of unequal length, hearing difficulties, arthritic conditions, eye ailments, back problems, migraine headaches, and various stages of cancer.

In these areas, with these conditions, one must be honest and acknowledge that there are times when such ailments are affected by variables beyond a person's faith. A fall with resulting blow on the head has restored sight to a blind person; a sneeze has relieved a deaf condition; and astronaut Donald (Deke) Slayton's abnormal heartbeat did mysteriously disappear.

And one must always be conscious that not all of man's physical pain and distress rest in malfunctioning of tangible muscle, ligament, or organ. To fail to observe and acknowledge this would do the cause of divine healing irreparable harm.

In so saying, I am not offering an "excuse" or "alternative" for the divine healing that is experienced. I am not trying to normalize the miracle. Nor am I placing Jesus in the clever role of a magician, a hypnotist who lived far in advance of His time.

Jesus was the Son of God, miraculously born, miraculously raised from the dead, the Man who had that divine touch of healing that staunched the woman's issue of blood, that poured new life into atrophied muscles.

As I raise the point that not all cases of "divine healing" are divine healing, I seek to shake no man's faith. Surely not all cases where God heals a deaf man can be attributed to Eustachian tubes that became unplugged as a result of a two-dollar sneeze. I would simply point out that Christians can draw faulty conclusions from insufficient data. Christians are human.

In one sense, acknowledged by many physicians, all healing is divine. Yet, we have sought to present in this book cases that show God at work beyond the normal healing of tissues. And we see clearly in several cases that some may question, the miracle of perfect timing, instances when God's will and man's thinking intersected at a peculiar moment of healing, a miracle in itself.

As a Christian who believes in Romans 8:28, I do not care to use the words "chance," "luck," or "fate" in my explanation of what happens to me. My God is not Someone who has me spin a roulette wheel, allowing the pointer to stop at random on the red or black, a chance number. My God controls where the wheel stops. The game is fixed.

I have been disappointed, yet understanding, of the medical field's reluctance to place their stamp of approval and acceptance upon divine healing. The number of M.D., D.O., D.D.S., and Ph.D., witnesses to the account in this book is slim. I sense the pressure upon a person trained in science, especially the healing arts, to remain completely scientific. The field of healing is certainly not without its quackery. Pseudo-healers have preyed upon the public, promulgating untold misery by encouraging ill people to leave acceptable medical treatment and drink their "miracle solutions" as they sit in "radioactive mines."

My respect for science, my involvement in it, my acceptance of the methods it represents, help me understand the reluctance of highly trained people to admit divine healing. I am convinced, however, that in divine healing we have something different, something authentic, something that lies beyond $E = MC^2$.

Nevertheless, I know that the opinion of a medical doctor, a qualified surgeon, a recognized specialist carries a great deal of weight. Hence their notable absence from this book is bound to be disappointing to many readers.

God asks different things of different people, calling us to a wide range of skills, allowing us to have a variety of mind sets, and yet makes it possible for us to fellowship together at the foot of the cross. His death upon that cross can heal such differences in our thinking, permitting us to accept and be acceptable in that Christian fellowship.

And that in itself is another healing miracle.

Praise God!

A PARTING WORD TO SKEPTICS AND TO BELIEVERS

The person who has read the testimonies in this book will be left with one of several feelings. I doubt if many readers will find their mental gears idling in neutral, having no opinion concerning the case histories of people who claim that God has healed them. We either raise our eyebrows in question, or our eyes glow in confirmation.

For the Eyebrow Raisers

Undoubtedly some readers will shift into reverse and furiously backpedal away from these odd, weird experiences. Likely a number of those who smile at the naivity of the healed were skeptics at the beginning. Long before they read this book, they had placed God in a box.

Their God was of a certain size, with certain limitations. Their feelings toward those who testify of divine healing are the feelings one has of those who are misled by religious sects.

Skeptics can be kind; they can be cruel. They may be prejudiced. They are often highly educated men and women who think deeply and clearly within the boundaries that they have set up as limitations upon their God. I respect the skeptic. I would like the skeptic to respect me, to respect the person in this book who says simply, "God healed me."

To believe in divine healing is not a condition for salvation. How thankful we are that God accepts us on the basis of our belief in the healing work of Jesus on the cross, not His healing work in our physical body. What counts is what we think of the Galilean Physician who heals our souls, not what we think of the cases cited in this book.

My suggestions to the eyebrow raisers are few in number. Faith comes in various hues, in assorted sizes. We make our choice of that faith and adapt ourselves to it. When my mother purchased clothes for us children, she usually took the next size larger than what fit us at the time. It was a bit sloppy, but it allowed us to "grow into it." Sometimes we need to pick a faith that allows for expansion. Too small a faith constricts, even hurts. Certainly it limits.

My second suggestion to the skeptic is more of a plea. Perhaps you cannot visualize God as a healing God, but in the fellowship of believers there are those who do see God as the provider of that fragrant balm from Gilead. Accept us who feel that we have so been blessed. Some in the kingdom may need a fuller revelation of God's mercy in order to believe in the same Lord. In one sense, we may be the weaker brethren. Accept us.

For the Eye Glowers

And now a word to those of us who emerge from the reading of this book with a song of praise on our lips. Let others hear that song. It is not a song that glorifies the singer, not a praise that honors the praiser, but a melody that exalts our risen Savior who conquered death itself.

Let us be neither ignorant nor omnipotent in our opinion. Let us neither be reluctant or belligerent in our testimony. Let us not be ashamed to acknowledge that our God is a God of perfect timing. In the fullness of time He sent His healing Son, not before, not after, but at the exact moment in history when it fitted best into God's overall design.

And so healing from God comes at His moment, not ours. To pray, "Not my will, but Thine be done," is not a phrase of escape, our excuse to cover us when healing does not come. God needs no alibis. Instead the phrase is uttered as acknowledgment of our submission to a God who knows best, whose knowledge transcends our limited powers of thinking, who sees the whole, not the part.

Let us not deny that our God is a Healer of the mind, of the emotions, where many of our physical ailments originate. When some sneer as they point out that many of our illnesses are psychosomatic in nature, that they rest in the mind, that divine healing is only the result of a new "mind set," let us not violently disagree. To heal the neurons is no mean thing. Our God is a God of miracles, a God of order, a God who ministers to us through the complex and the simple.

Death Comes to the Healed

By the time this book is published, some of those who testified of healing may have gone to be with the Lord. And some may carry on their death certificate as the reason for their decease, the very disease to which they testify of having been healed. It is like the brother who said in connection with his healing, "Although I know that I have been healed of this disease, healed by God, it does not mean that I will not be visited again by it. If God spares me from death in an automobile accident in my youth, it does not mean that I am divinely protected for the rest of my life from any injury involving an internal combustion engine. I simply praise Him for that first deliverance, for the extended life." My friend had been healed of cancer and smiled as he gave his testimony.

If such a simple submission to God's will is too marshmallowy for the reader, then I am sorry for the reader. I find it easier to submit to an infallible God than to a limited man.

Death Comes to All

As a believer in divine healing, one does not pray for eternal life. We already have it. We do not insist that God continually delay our time of transition from this earthly realm below to the heavenly courts above. We simply live in the plentitude of His grace, knowing that it is sufficient, eternal. God does not limit His grace to us while upon this earth. Death does not mark a cessation of that grace. A terminal illness does not terminate.

The last sentence above is an understandable paradox for the Christian who believes in divine healing. What is identified as physical death simply marks a tiny iota of time that moves us from the hot plains below where the mercy drops sprinkle down on these fading bodies of ours to the cool valleys beyond where His continual showers of grace cause us to blossom and bloom eternally in His blessed presence.

Again, Divine Healing Is Not by Formula

To be spiritually made whole is an unbeatable experience. To be physically healed by God is also a blessed event. Neither are scientifically explainable. We have come to accept the first; the second seems a bit more scary, even untenable for some. How strange.

Divine healing is not an emotional experience, yet no formula can be given to guarantee its happening. The route we know, but the destination is not always attainable. For reasons we do not know, God at times detours us, at times says, "I'm sorry, but I have other plans for you than to heal your ailment." You have read of such cases in this book.

God seems to demand a certain transparency from the one who seeks divine healing, not a token submission, but surrender so total that only a vacuum remains. It is a vacuum that God fills as He sees fit. And so if the healing comes, or if the cancer remains, there is still victory. The excision of self is major surgery. There have been no deaths from such an operation.

Divine healing suggests to me that we place ourselves before God and pray, *"Giver and Sustainer of life, heal me if it is Your will. Heal me for a moment, for a year, for a decade, for an age. Heal me partially; heal me completely. Heal me through the physician, the surgeon, the therapist who has mastered the wisdom of man so freely given by God. Heal me by the hand of Your minister, Your lay servant, the one to whom You have handed the gift of healing. Heal me through the Comforter, the Holy Spirit Who came to replace Your Son, the One who made the blind to see, the deaf to hear, the lame to walk. And even as the Holy Spirit was intended to glorify Christ, so let me glorify Him as I experience Your healing work in my life. Amen and amen."*

ADDRESSES

Brenneman, Helen Good
516 E. Waverly Avenue
Goshen, IN 46526
"Enabling Grace"

Bustos, Margarito
1423 Mississippi Avenue
Davenport, IA 52803
"Healed at Communion"

Buzzard, Harold
1800 Stevens Avenue
Elkhart, IN 46514
"I Live in a World of Light"

Dalton, Sue
25761 Alexander
Bedford, OH 44146
   "Everyday Is Hallelujah Day at Our House"

Denlinger, Marilyn
1519 N. College Avenue
Harrisonburg, VA 22801
   "This Child Should Have Died"

Graber, Carolyn
Route 1
Plymouth, IN 46563
   "Histoplasmosis and Amphotericin B"

Hart, Elizabeth
Box 534, Route 4
Manheim, PA 17545
   "Healed and in a Wheelchair"

Heatwole, Linda
120 Sproul Lane
Staunton, VA 24401
   "We Prayed for Our Son—and He Lived"

Hostetler, S. Jay
2000 S. 15th Street
Goshen, IN 46526
   "Both Daughter and Mother"

Kanagy, Nelson
3826 Royal Palm Avenue
Sarasota, FL 33580
   "Perhaps a Year"

Lapp, Rhoda S.
1612 Morningside Drive
Lancaster, PA 17602
   "The Nurse Who Was Healed"

Martin, Lois
Route 1
Kinzer, PA 17535
   "The Diagnosis Was Leukemia"

Martin, Ruth
357 S. San Antonio
Upland, CA 91786
   "Healed Without Asking"

Miller, Ella May
1312 College Avenue
Harrisonburg, VA 22801
   "Twice Anointed, Twice Healed"

Miller, Glen Dale
Route 1, Box 252
Middlebury, IN 46540
   "We Call It a Miracle"

Miller, Kate M.
1528 S. Tuttle Avenue
Sarasota, FL 33580
   "Rise Up and Walk"

Otto, John
111 S. 13th Street
Fort Dodge, IA 50501
   "Lumps in the Abdomen"

Roth, Nelson R.
204 Spring Street
Martinsburg, PA 16662
  "Hospital Bed to Pulpit"

Schumm, Clare F.
322 Concord Avenue
Elkhart, IN 46514
  "Let God's Healing Power Be Released"

Shank, John W.
1095 Shenandoah Avenue
Harrisonburg, VA 22801
  "The Double Cure"

Swartzendruber, Alva
Pleasantville Home
Kalona, IA 52240
  "From Confinement to Freedom"

Witmer, Robert
249 Av. De La Division-Leclerc
92 Chatenay-Malabry,
France
  "The 'Moth Eaten' Illium"

Yoder, Ora M. and Grace
Box 245
Shipshewana, IN 46565
  "We Prayed for Our Son—and He Died"

Zimmerman, Harvey R.
R.D. 1
East Earl, PA 17519
  "My Delayed Healing"

SELECTED BIBLIOGRAPHY*

Bingham, Rowland, *The Bible and the Body*, Holborn, England, Marshall Morgan, 1939.

Boggs, Wade H., Jr., *Faith Healing and the Christian Faith*, Virginia, John Knox Press, 1956.

Bonnell, John Sutherland, *Do You Want to Be Healed?*, New York, Harper and Row, 1968.

Bowman, Warren, *Anointing for Healing*, Elgin, Illinois, The Brethren Press, 1942.

Gross, Don H., *The Case for Spiritual Healing*, New York, Nelson, 1958.

Hulme, William E., *Dialogue in Despair*, New York, Abingdon, 1968.

Ikin, A. Graham, *New Concepts of Healing*, New York, Associated Press, 1956

Kraus, Norman C., *The Healing Christ*, Scottdale, Pennsylvania, Herald Press, 1972.

Macleod, George F., *The Place of Healing in the Ministry of the Church*, Glasgow, Scotland, The Iona Community Publishing Department.

Martin, Bernard, *Healing for You*, Virginia, John Knox Press, 1965.

Miller, Paul M., *How God Heals*, Scottdale, Pennsylvania, Herald Press, 1960 (revised edition scheduled for publication in 1975).

Oates, Wayne E., *The Revelation of God in Human Suffering*, Philadelphia, Westminster Press, 1959.

Orr, William R., *Does God Heal Today?*, Illinois, Van Kampen Press.

Oursler, Will, *The Healing Power of Faith*, New York, Hawthorn, 1957.

Westberg, Granger, *Where Minister and Doctor Meet*, New York, Harper, 1961.

Woods, Nellie E., *The Healing of the Bible*, New York, Hawthorn, 1958.

*Excerpted from more exhaustive bibliographies on divine healing compiled by Paul M. Miller, Mennonite Biblical Seminary, Elkhart, Indiana.

THE AUTHOR

Robert J. Baker, a native of the Hoosier state, was born in Goshen, Indiana, and has lived for many years in nearby Elkhart. He received the BA degree from Goshen College, Goshen, Indiana; the MS degree from Indiana University, Bloomington, Indiana; and the MAT degree from Michigan State University, East Lansing, Michigan. He completed further graduate training at Emory University, Atlanta, Georgia, and the Indiana State University, Terre Haute, Indiana.

His first written material was published in 1937 in a school anthology for students at Elkhart High School. Hundreds of his short stories, articles and poems have appeared in the religious press during the past thirty-five years, frequently under a pseudonym. *Second Chance,* a book of his short stories, was released by Herald Press in 1968. He has served as associate editor of the *Gospel Evangel* for more than a decade and his weekly column for Sunday school teachers has appeared in *Builder* since January, 1965.

Married and the father of five, Mr. Baker has taught on the junior high level for the Elkhart Community Schools for twenty-five years. He worships at the Belmont Mennonite Church of Elkhart where he has been an active layman for the past forty years.